Black Resistance in High School

SUNY Series,
FRONTIERS IN EDUCATION
Philip G. Altbach, Editor

The Frontiers in Education Series draws upon a range of disciplines and approaches in the analysis of contemporary educational issues and concerns. Books in the series help to reinterpret established fields of scholarship in education by encouraging the latest synthesis and research. A special focus highlights educational policy issues from a multidisciplinary perspective. The series is published in cooperation with the Graduate School of Education, State University of New York at Buffalo.

Black Resistance in High School
Forging a Separatist Culture

R. Patrick Solomon

Foreword by John U. Ogbu

State University of New York Press

Published by
State University of New York Press, Albany

For information, address State University of New York
Press, State University Plaza, Albany, N.Y. 12246

Production by Dana Foote
Marketing by Fran Keneston

Library of Congress Cataloging-in-Publication Data

Solomon, Rovell Patrick.
      Black resistance in high school : forging a separatist culture /
   R. Patrick Solomon ; with a foreword by John U. Ogbu.
            p.   cm. — (SUNY series, frontiers in education)
      Includes bibliographical references and index.
            ISBN 0–7914-0847–7 (alk. paper) . — ISBN 0–7914-0848–5 (pkb. :
   alk. paper)
            1. Students, Black—Ontario—Toronto—Social conditions—Case
   studies. 2. West Indians—Education—Ontario—Toronto—Case
   studies. I. Title. II. Series
   LC2804.2.06S66   1992
   373.18' 2969729' 0713—dc20
                                                                    90–24847
                                                                          CIP

10 9 8 7 6 5 4 3 2 1

Contents

JOHN U. OGBU

Foreword

Minority groups in modern urban industrial societies experience many difficulties using formal education to achieve upward social mobility. This is true in Britain, Canada, France, Japan, New Zealand, the United States, and West Germany. The disproportionate school failure of minority-group children has become one of the most active research issues in education as researchers attempt to understand the underlying causes and to provide policymakers and educators with reliable and useful information. Competing theories have arisen out of this research enterprise, and Patrick Solomon's book is both a good case study of how minorities fail to achieve upward social mobility through education and a contribution to the theory of why they fail.

The author studied the school experience of West Indian children in a high school in Metropolitan Toronto, Canada. Using an ethnographic method he examined the position of the West Indian community in Toronto's socioeconomic hierarchy, and the reasons why they occupy such an unenviable position. Like most immigrants, West Indians in Toronto suffered a loss in status—which they initially accepted—hoping that through education their children would get more decent and better-paying jobs. This expected intergenerational mobility, Dr. Solomon's research revealed, will not be realized for the group he studied.

The author shows how the school contributes to the failure of the children through its tracking and curriculum placement policies as well as through the way it controls the students. He also shows how the victim contributes to his own victimization: West Indian children bring to school certain attitudes and behaviors that are not necessarily conducive to scholastic success. In addition, the children respond to their treatment by the school in a manner that compounds their problem: they form separatist groups, they refuse to follow school rules about the use of time and space, they are over-involved in sports almost to the exclusion of their schoolwork, and so on. The combined effect of the actions of the school and the children's "lived culture" is that the children fail, in spite of their expressed desire to succeed in school.

This book is also about the theories explaining minority school failure, especially the social reproduction and resistance theories or, as the author puts it, the structuralist and the culturalist perspectives. Structuralists focus on the structural regularities or requirements and actions of the system. Structuralists generally conclude that working-class children fail in school because the structured social relations within the school teach them to "take their place" within a class-based hierarchy in a capitalist system. Culturalists, on the other hand, focus on students and their "self-created and lived culture" in the school setting. In Dr. Solomon's study, the latter include students' cultural behaviors, language, mode of dress, and involvement in sports. This "antischool" orientation and behavior is interpreted by culturalists as a means of conscious or unconscious resistance against the system. The author concludes that we need both the structuralist and the culturalist perspectives in order to more fully understand minority school failure.

Reproduction and resistance theorists have generally used social class as the basis for their analysis and explanation. Proponents, with few exceptions, assume that the foundation for social reproduction through schooling is social class, not race, ethnicity, or gender. They tend to treat the educational problems of ethnic/racial minorities as if they are the same as those of the working-class members of the dominant group. This preoccupation with class is not surprising, given the Marxist orientation of many structuralists and culturalists. In my view, these scholars have a rather simplistic notion of the problem, seeing it as if it were only a matter of socioeconomic inequality.

Dr. Solomon tells us that on the basis of his own findings and evidence from other studies, race must be taken into account in developing a meaningful theory of social reproduction through schooling. The reason is that studies, including his own, have revealed important areas in which the experience and behaviors of racial minority students differ from those of the working-class members of the dominant group. One difference is that the minority students generally "affirm schooling," whereas the working-class students from the dominant group "flatly reject the achievement ideology" through schooling. Yet, in spite of their acceptance of the legitimacy of obtaining good school credentials as the means to good jobs with decent pay, the minorities behave in a manner that makes it difficult for them to attain their educational and employment goals. Why does this paradox of high educational aspiration and low school performance exist? We do not yet have a satisfactory answer to this question.

There are other unanswered questions partly raised by the present study. One such question is why social reproduction does not occur among all racial minorities who suffered a loss in their socioeconomic status. In Britain, Canada, and the United States, for example, there are immigrant minorities who initially suffered status reduction and yet their children, through schooling, achieved upward social mobility. What makes them different from West Indian immigrants in this study whose children did not become upwardly mobile?

Furthermore, we now have studies of West Indians in Britain, Canada, the Virgin Islands, and the continental U.S., and they seem to have different school experiences in these places. From these studies we have determined that West Indians are successful in school in the Virgin Islands and in the continental U.S., but not in Britain or Canada. In both the Virgin Islands and in the U.S., West Indians generally do better in school than the "native black Americans" and it appears that the status of the first generation is not reproduced through schooling in the second generation. Why?

I suggest that the answer may lie partly in the terms of the incorporation of minorities into a given society and partly in the way the minority group defines its status: as immigrants or "foreigners" (e.g., West Indians in the Virgin Islands and the U.S.) or as citizens, colonials, or members of the "commonwealth" with certain rights and privileges (e.g., West Indians in Britain and Canada). The self-definition of minorities as "foreigners" or "citizens" has important implications for the way the minorities perceive and respond to their treatment in school and society.

Finally, the concepts of "opposition" and "resistance" need to be more refined when applied to the educational problems of racial minorities. No doubt the phenomena of both opposition and resistance exist in the minority populations, but may not be necessarily directed at schooling, even though they adversely affect schooling. A good example of this is the case of a group of college women who arrived at the college with high aspirations for school success and high hopes for professional careers. However, while in college they "constructed a peer culture" in which the preoccupation was securing male companionship. It was to this end that the women invested their time and effort, and in doing so "derailed" their academic and professional pursuits. Reproduction thus occurred without the interference of the structural regularities of the school and without any apparent conflict between the women and the system, let alone resistance on the part of the students.

Among racial minorities, especially involuntary minorities (i.e., minorities who were incorporated into a society against their will through slavery, colonization, or conquest), there have usually been episodes in their histories resulting in their formation of an oppositional group identity and an oppositional cultural frame of reference vis-à-vis the group identity and cultural frame of reference of the dominant group. For these minorities there appears to coexist an opposing dual cultural frame of reference: one frame of reference or proper way to behave is regarded as appropriate only for dominant-group members; the other cultural frame of reference is more appropriate for the minorities.

All minority groups go to school with some degree of cultural and language differences, including differences in cultural frames of reference. However, it is the involuntary minorities who have greater difficulty crossing cultural and language boundaries at school and are generally less successful.

The reason appears to lie in the way the two types of minorities, voluntary and involuntary, interpret their cultural and language differences.

Voluntary minorities interpret these differences as barriers to be overcome in order to achieve their social and economic goals. These minorities selectively learn the language and other cultural features or practices of the school, without imagining that this requires them to give up their own minority language and culture. That is, they don't perceive a threat to their minority language or cultural identity.

For involuntary minorities, the situation is different. In contrast, they interpret their cultural and language differences as markers or symbols of a group identity to be maintained, not as a barrier to be overcome. And because of this interpretation, they do not appear to make a clear distinction, as voluntary minorities do, between what they have to learn or do to enhance their school success (for example, learning and using the standard English and standard behaviors of the school) and what they must do to maintain their minority cultural frame of reference and identity distinct from that of their "oppressors."

Racial minorities who are involuntary minorities understand that school success and good school credentials are necessary for getting jobs with decent pay. They accept the legitimacy of upward mobility through schooling, although they wish the principle or rule applied to them to the same degree it applies to their dominant-group peers. The paradox of their aspirations and low performance arises partly from two factors. One is that while they want education for employment, they also realize that as racial minorities school credentials are necessary but not sufficient for their advancement. Consequently, these minorities divert some of their time, resources, and effort to the pursuit of alternative or survival strategies (for example, sports). This reduces their investment in education and affects their chances of school success. Furthermore, because they consciously and unconsciously interpret their cultural and language differences as symbols of identity to be maintained, they also consciously or unconsciously oppose or avoid learning and using the standard English and certain school cultural practices, perceiving them as a threat to their own minority cultural and language identity. In other words, because of the meaning that these minorities give to their cultural and language difference, they have a greater tendency to classify such school requirements as regular attendance, being on time, paying attention in class, doing schoolwork and homework regularly, persevering in one's academic work, and the like as a part of the cultural frame of reference of the dominant group and not for minorities.

I need to emphasize that the interpretation of cultural and language differences is something that evolved historically and not just a creation of minority children in their present school setting. Once this interpretation has become an ingrained part of the minority culture it affects even the very young who lack the understanding of the labor market and their parents' experiences within it. Of course, as the children get older and become more aware of their group's status mobility system, they begin to perceive and use the cultural and language differences more or less consciously to "resist" or "oppose" what they do not like in school, because they perceive the school as an institution of the dominant group.

I dare say that there are "resistance" theorists who seem to romanticize the "antischool" behaviors of some racial minority youths. Many of these young people do not really know why they behave the way they do. Nor do they understand the full consequences of their behaviors. I suggest that the way to help these young people to avoid reproducing their parents' menial status is to show them that following school rules of behavior for achievement (for example, regular school attendance, doing school and home work, paying attention in class, etc.) does not require them to give up their own minority cultural frame of reference. We do not help these young people by telling them that we admire and encourage their "resistance" to the system. Rather, we should show them how to succeed by practicing accommodation without assimilation. This is what most successful minorities do, and Dr. Solomon's book provides us with many insights of what can be done.

Acknowledgments

I gratefully acknowledge the contributions of many individuals who have supported this project, in many different ways, from its inception to its completion. First and foremost, I would like to thank my dissertation advisor and mentor, Lois Weis, who recognized the importance of this work and helped me work through emerging themes from my fieldwork, and establish their relevance to the current theories in the Sociology of Education. Maxine Seller and Edward Herberg helped mold the project at its dissertation stage, while John Ogbu and Phil Altbach provided the much-needed guidance in moving the work from dissertation to book.

My colleagues, Ahmed Ijaz, Sabra Desai, Delroy Louden, Allan Fairbridge, Howard Palmer, Norma Sommerville, and others working with me in the Canadian race relations minefield, all deserve acknowledgment for their support in this venture. I am very thankful for the word processing skills and the patience of Patricia Porter, Sybil Downer, Una Pinnock, and Christopher Solomon who worked, usually under time constraints, on successive drafts of the manuscript. Lois Patton and her staff at the SUNY Press provided penetrating critiques and useful suggestions for the improvement of this book. Special thanks to the students, staff, and parents of Lumberville, and especially the Jocks, for accepting me into their "inner circle" and sharing with me their thoughts, frustrations, and aspirations. Ethical considerations prevent me from identifying them by name. Finally, my greatest debt of gratitude goes to my son Christopher and my wife Sylvia whose emotional and moral support sustained me through my various roles as doctoral candidate, field researcher, and writer.

Patrick Solomon

CHAPTER 1

Black Cultural Forms in Schools

> Subcultures (thus) are not isolated from the powerful; their culture is set in relation to the dominant cultures surrounding them...
> (Quantz & O'Connor, 1988)

Over the years student groups with distinctive cultures have forged varied relationships with school structures. These subgroups have ranged from those that are fully integrated into the social system to others that are profoundly antischool. The "conformists" or "mainstreamers," for example, obey school rules, show respect for authority, conform to expectations, and are generally supportive of the authority structure of their school. At the other extreme, however, are student subcultures that are expressedly nonconformist and antischool. Their lived experiences, system of practices, and way of life differ from those of students of the dominant culture. As a result, conflict and tension characterize their relationship with school authority as they break school rules, disregard the codes of conduct, and strive to impose their own values, beliefs, and dispositions on the dominant school culture. It is this point of conflict that produces antagonistic relationships that have in recent years become the focus of many educational researchers. Ethnographic studies carried out within schools provide good insights into how dominant and subordinate cultures struggle for control of these institutions.

This book is about such a struggle. It documents and analyzes the oppositional relationship between a black student subculture and the authority structure of a Canadian high school. The influx of black immigrants into Canada over the past two decades exposed its school system to a student culture that was different from the predominantly white mainstream culture. The cohesive group of black, working-class, West Indian immigrant boys in this study, socially differentiated from the dominant culture in many ways, became a substantial challenge to the white, middle-class school structure. As we shall see, such a student group does not operate arbitrarily; the culture they generate is influenced by such powerful factors as their social class, race, ethnicity,

1

and immigrant status. For example, Willis's (1977) ethnography highlighted a British student subculture influenced by social class. The "lads," as Willis calls them, actively differentiated themselves from the dominant middle-class bias of the school and spent their time engaged in counterschool activities, creating diversions and enjoyment, avoiding work, "having a laff," and skill-fully working the system. Conflicts and tensions pervaded the interaction between these lads and the school staff. What were the reasons for such coun-terschool behaviors? Willis concludes that working-class students engage in subcultural activities because they realize that conformism for their class is fruitless; schooling will not improve their life chances. So they generate behaviors that not only give them social power, but affirm their acceptance of their subordinate economic fate like their parents before them.

In addition to class-based oppositional forms, gender-based subcultures are important at their point of intersection with the black, working-class male subculture in this study. While McRobbie (1978) and Griffin's (1985) research on British working-class girls showed that females contest class and patriarchal forms of domination they encounter at home, school, and in the workplace, Fuller's (1980) study of black girls in a London comprehensive school added the dynamic of race to such interaction. She found that the rather obvious Anglocentric and middle-class biases in the structure, organi-zation, and curriculum of the school made it a battleground of opposing val-ues; a terrain where black girls demonstrate their resistance to class, gender, and ethnoracial values with which they do not identify. The challenges that fill the relationship between black males and females in Fuller's 1982 British study appear to have their origin in the group's differential commitment to a West Indian social formation characterized by male dominance. These intra-group tensions are of particular significance to the understanding of black females' accommodation and resistance to the domination of black male sub-cultural behaviors in this Canadian study. How different are black cultural forms from those of whites, and will the patterns of working-class West Indi-an blacks in Canadian schools be different from those of other blacks in U.S. and British schools?

BLACK CULTURAL FORMS IN SCHOOLS

While the dynamic of race is still conspicuously underemployed in theories on schooling and resistance to the reproduction of inequality, emerging research in the U.S. and Britain is becoming more sensitive to its signifi-cance to some subordinate cultures. The earlier literature on minority-group response to the content and process of schooling viewed black subcultures from a psychosocial perspective. Black pathology and social deviance were explained in terms of the inadequacy of the black family to cope in white society. Gradually, however, conflict theorists gained prominence in interpreting black oppositional forms as a political response to the white, middleclass organization of the school. This gradual redefinition has given new meaning to terms such as "black power," "black rebellion," and "black culture of resistance." What then is the nature of black oppositional forms at the point of conflict?

Studies of black students culture in U.S. schools have documented a range of attitudes and a repertoire of behaviors that are perceived as characteristic of black culture. Gilmore's (1985) study of black elementary students, for example, described their "stylized sulking" and "doin' steps" as statements of open resistance to the ethos of the school and a challenge to teacher authority. "Stylized sulking" is described by Gilmore as rather disgruntled nonverbal postures and facial expressions, and "doin' steps" as a steady alternating rhythm of foot stepping and hand clapping. Teachers and school administrators see these student activities as part of a stereotypic, communicative style of black culture and interpret them as bad attitude, defiance, insolence, and insubordination. They were associated with black vernacular "street" culture, and banned by school administrations as being lewd, disrespectful, and "inappropriate for school." Gilmore sees such an institutional response to these cultural forms as "containing the children's symbolic social portraits of the dynamic of schooling" (p.124).

At the high school level, the research of Petroni (1970) and Fordham and Ogbu (1986) found striking similarities in the practices and symbolism of black culture in U.S. schools. The students that Petroni studied painstakingly defined and monitored "black activities" to ensure their separation from "white activities." By wearing symbols of black identity such as the "Afro" hairstyle and engaging in discourses on "black power," black students created a sense of separateness in intergroup relations. In addition, students who embraced the black cultural identity disassociated themselves from both curricular and extracurricular activities they perceived as white. Powerful negative sanctions such as name-calling and labels of "Uncle Toms" and "white negroes" were brought to bear on black students who did not conform to "black ways." However, participation in activities such as athletics, perceived as the blacks' domain, received high recognition from fellow blacks. While these cultural forms were not overtly oppositional to school ethos, they were symbolic of a rebellion against the established social order. In addition, a differential commitment to black cultural behaviors gave rise to intragroup conflicts, especially between those who strove for black identity and others who gravitated toward the white, mainstream culture.

Fordham and Ogbu's (1986) ethnographic study of black students in an urban, predominantly black high school found elements of opposition and resistance against what they perceived as the prerogative of white Americans. Embracing the school curriculum and such attendant activities as speaking standard English, spending a lot of time in the library, working hard to get good grades, and being on time were perceived as "acting white." Here again, black students who engaged in academic pursuits were labeled "brainiacs" and were alienated, ostracized, or even physically assaulted by militant blacks. In their effort to develop, express, and maintain a black cultural identity, students engaged in a number of practices that were often in conflict with school norms. They were opposed to, and actively resisted, for themselves and their black peers, any behaviors they perceived as "acting white."

Black lower-class cultural behaviors that operated in opposition to the American high school structure were vividly documented in the research by Marotto (1977) and Foster (1986). The activities of the "Boulevard Brothers" in Marotto's ethnography conflicted with the expectations of their white peers, teachers, and the authority structure of their school. Their street corner behavior repertoire and life-style included such activities as the manipulation of others, flouting school rules, noninvolvement in academic pursuits, and preserving group cohesion and identity through their style of dress and demeanor. Through their informal networks they not only generated social power, but effectively circumvented the school's maintenance system. The authority structure responded with exasperation and consternation, neglecting, suspending and failing the "Brothers." Marotto's analysis of this confrontation between student culture and school structure is summarized thus:

> The school denies the students freedom, masses and fails to differentiate them, keeps them powerless and in a state of spectatorship, provides little human interaction and gives them primarily future oriented and symbolic rewards; the group's street corner frame of reference gave the Brothers independence of action and the immediate pleasure of participating in human interaction. (p.5)

Foster (1986) interprets some aspects of the culture and life-style of black lower-class adolescent males as socially approved behaviors perfected for their own survival in a hostile, urban, street corner environment. The verbal games of "Ribbin', Jivin', and Playin' the Dozens" are survival strategies designed to manipulate, persuade, and even accommodate others, including school authority figures. Verbal and nonverbal language are used by these blacks to give the impression of subservience to authority while at the same time controlling and concealing their true emotions. Street corner rituals institutionalized in the black lower-class American culture are seen as rebelliously inappropriate and a disruptive influence when practiced in schools. Teachers' refusal to tolerate this life-style resulted in tension-filled confrontations with black students. At the community college level, black student culture takes on a more contradictory element. As Weis (1985) shows, black cultural forms affirm the process of education on one hand, but students practiced contradictory behaviors such as dropping in and out of school and exerting little effort in their academic tasks.

From these profiles of black cultural forms in all levels of American educational institutions have emerged some key insights into why student cultures conflict with school structures. Certain attitudes, rituals, and styles of behavior, perceived as characteristic of black culture, solidify black identity and at the same time alienate the dominant-group culture. Because these behaviors are at variance with the established social order, indulgent students come into conflict with the authority structure of the school. Why have these students shown no vested interest in maintaining a white-dominated school structure? Ogbu (1974) and Weis (1985) argue that the relationship of blacks and whites in the larger American society is historically rooted. Blacks' unequal and subordinate socioeconomic position in the U.S. and their struggle to extricate themselves from this disadvantaged position has given rise to student oppositional cultures that are historically informed. For example, Genovese (1974) explains that black slaves developed a culture of resistance to the institution of slavery and demonstrated their opposition through their language and communication patterns, their work rhythms, and their frequent running away from the burden of slavery. As Weis (1985:134) analyzed it, "These oppositional practices have been lived out and elaborated upon over the years, and constitute core cultural elements in the urban black community today." Black cultural forms within U.S. schools are often responses to what Ogbu and Weis see as explicit in the system: the cost of being black is that whites get greater rewards for any given amount of schooling than non-whites. This realization, Weis concludes, has "fostered the reproduction of deeply rooted race-class antagonisms in the broader society" (1986:14).

An overview of black oppositional forms within schools would be incomplete without an analysis of the development of the black youth culture in Britain. When West Indians migrated to Britain, they did so largely to increase the possibilities of both educational and occupational mobility. They were prepared to compromise and to be politically cautious in the host country. Second-generation West Indian youth, however, became defined as constituting a culture of resistance, engaging in ecstatic life-styles, and abstracting themselves from their marginalized positions in British society. A plethora of research captured a range of these cultural forms: readopting creole as a form of linguistic resistance, differential use of reggae music and its associated life-style, celebration of masculinity; street hustling and a refusal to work; and embracing Rastafarian beliefs and spreading oppositional messages.[1]

Researchers such as Wood (1974) Pryce (1978) see the cultural life-styles of the larger black community as a response or an orientation to social situations in which they find themselves. Their studies utilized the life-style concepts adapted from Hannerz's (1969) research of the black ghetto culture and community in the United States. The distinctive styles of existence for these black West Indians in Britain ranged from the status-aspiring "mainstreamers" or "mainliner" to the antiestablishment "teenyboppers." Pryce saw the mainliners as achievement oriented, qualifications-conscious, and motivated by the concerns of status and responsibility. By and large, mainliners are conformers who want to be integrated in the mainstream British society, and have no allegiance to culture-specific political groups. At the other extreme of the life-style spectrum are the teenyboppers, a male subculture that has dropped out of the mainstream, are usually unemployed, and quite often in conflict with the law. They reject the status quo, and are in conflict with the dominant white society for discriminating against them in education and employment. Later in life, the teenyboppers resort to a life-style of hustling—a disreputable way of life—to earn a living, and to avoid the drudgery of routinized, unskilled labor. This life-style, Hebdige (1976) and Brake (1980) conclude, was inspired by Rastafarian ideology and resistance messages disseminated in reggae music. These are the types of oppositional cultures with which black, working-class children experiment in their communities.

The expectation of a black explosion in British schools was based, in part, on black students' oppositional frame of reference from the larger black community. Dhondy's (1974) concern was also based on his observation of black students' challenge and rejection of school discipline, study, and routine: "a reaction to the discipline machine." He concluded that black students' culture of resistance was a response to the type of labor force for which the education system was preparing them. Later, Furlong's (1984) study of black resistance in a British comprehensive school found that black boys "drew selectively on popular culture, parental culture, and aspects of their institutional life in order to create their own unique cultural resistance" (p. 217). The boys' oppositional cultural forms included rude, aggressive, and confrontational styles of interaction with the staff. They invested time in exploiting the weaknesses of the school to create the social space for their group life. Furlong argued that although the boys took a contradictory approach to education, their culture of resistance developed only after they sensed they were failing academically, and wanted to maintain the myth of possibility of success. By the same token, Cashmore and Troyna (1982:7) believe that black youths' embracement of oppositional cultures, for example, the Rastafarian subculture, has some of its beginnings within schools:

> We see "the drift" as having its genesis not in the postschool experiences,
> as some commentators have insisted, but in the later stages of their secondary school education.

What factors within British schools, and the society at large, have given rise to West Indian oppositional and even counterschool cultures? Willis (1977:49) refers to "patterns of racial culture" and describes racism as embedded in the formal as well as the informal structures of school culture:

> Both [white] lads and staff do share their resentment for the [black] disconcerting intruder. For racism amongst the lads, it provides a double support

for hostile attitudes. The informal was, for once, backed up by at least the ghost of the formal.

Carby (1982) and Cashmore (1982) argue that the situation for black students in school was an extension of the situation the whole West Indian community faced socially in British society. Therefore, Cashmore (1982:184) concludes, forms of resistance in school must be understood within the wider context of the struggles against discrimination faced by the whole black community: "students practising forms of resistance as members of the black fraction of the working class."

How do black cultural forms in British schools compare with those in American schools? First, there are striking similarities in patterns of association. Establishing a group identity based on color and preserving group cohesion appear to be a key feature of this culture. Identity and group cohesion were maintained by in-group linguistic codes and communication patterns. The uniqueness of "black language" in the U.S. and West Indian "dialect" in Britain made it difficult for dominant-group students and teachers to participate in the communication process. In addition to the alienating effects of these language forms, popular black music such as "rap" and "reggae" was used to disseminate oppositional messages. Dress and demeanor also featured prominently in black identity, and are often a source of conflict between students and teachers. The literature also revealed that in both British and American schools there is differential commitment to black cultural identity. Black mainstreamers buy into school rules and regularities and support the status quo. Students who gravitate to more oppositional cultures spend a great deal of time opposing authority, being confrontational, and investing very little time and effort in their school work. Social commentators see such behaviors as growing out of the culture of the larger black community and as resistance to the subordination that racial minorities face in these white societies. As Genovese (1974) and Weis (1985) argue, the U.S. race-class antagonism is historically rooted in slavery and reproduced through an ongoing dominant-subordinate relationship that has existed between the two groups over time. In the case of Britain, its history of colonialism created similar tensions between blacks and whites in the West Indies. These tensions were heightened when immigrants from these islands sought equality with white natives in British society. From this comparative overview it appears then that the history of relationships between blacks and whites in the wider society helps determine the nature of in-school relationships. According to Weis, history is also one of the factors responsible for the difference between black and white cultural forms. Weis (1985:132) explains:

> The fact that blacks constitute a castelike group in American society means that student culture will automatically take a somewhat different shape and form from that of the white working class. Student cultural forms is also affected by the nature of historic struggle for particular groups.

A second difference between black and white oppositional forms may be related to their level of acceptance of the achievement ideology. Willis's working-class lads and MacLeod's (1987) "Hallway Hangers," for example, are white subcultures that flatly reject any possibility of upward mobility through schooling and therefore found it less conflicting to engage in the oppositional activities in school. To the contrary, some black working-class subcultures studied by Weis (1985), MacLeod (1987), and Fuller (1980) have high aspirations of "making it," so it is with much inner conflict that they resist the process of schooling. MacLeod concludes that ethnicity plays a key role in determining black students' belief in their chances of achieving social and economic mobility in society. Identifying ethnicity as a factor in black response to the achievement ideology is significant to the study of West Indian immigrants and their expectations in the Canadian socioeconomic structure. Such expectations have become powerful forces in mediating relationships with school structures. How do West Indian cultural forms impact on the Canadian school structure?

Because of the relatively new impact of black immigrants on the Canadian scene, sustained research on black culture in Canadian schools is only just emerging. This study was predated by a few empirical but mostly speculative and journalistic accounts of the existence and impact of a black youth subculture within urban schools and communities. For example, the *Toronto Life* magazine (March 1981:72) carried the following impressions:

> In the areas of Toronto where the West Indian community is concentrated ...gangs of black kids can be found at any time of day, lounging about, smoking a joint, listening to reggae on somebody's radio, chatting.... They have dropped out of school, aren't very welcome at home...They exist almost entirely outside the mainstream of society (Siggin).

Such a description of aWest Indian youth subculture in Toronto does not speculate as to why these youngsters separate themselves from the dominant culture and no longer embrace schooling as an avenue for making it in Canadian society. Other social commentators, however, have offered wide-ranging explanations. One of the most popular is the traditional immigrant adjustment model that explains the difficulties of newcomers in overcoming the differences between their old and new cultures. The rate at which immigrants overcome these cultural discontinuities often relies on factors such as the coping strategies of the immigrant and the receptivity of the host environment. Other explanations of subcultural behaviors such as cultural deprivation and social deviance among West Indian immigrants locate the problem squarely on the shoulders of the individual with disregard for the negative effect of the institutional structures in which they live. This is what Ryan (1976) describes as "blaming the victim."

This study of working-class West Indian students in a Canadian high school provides a perspective that scrutinizes the interaction of culture and structure. Central to this formulation is the notion of culture and cultural politics: how students utilize ethno-specific behaviors to oppose the school structures they perceive as not serving their interest. Here, we will explore the interaction between the authoritative system of the school representing the dominant culture of the wider society, and the cultural forms of students with allegiances to the specific subgroup differentiated from the dominant culture by class, race, and immigrant status. What is it within schools that student subcultures oppose? And why are institutions of learning described as arenas where class, gender, and race antagonisms and meanings are lived out?

SCHOOLS AS ARENAS OF CONFLICT

From a review of the literature it appears as if student subcultures oppose school structures because of their hidden and formal curriculum. Some educational theorists such as Apple and Weis (1983) see schooling for working-class students as characterized by the tacit teaching of middle-class norms, values, and dispositions through institutional expectations and the routines of day-to-day school life. Working-class subcultures often oppose the rigid rules, the respect for external rewards, the orderly work habits, and the demand for subordination that schools sought in order to achieve these expectations. Theorists such as Parsons (1959) view the function of the hidden curriculum as a necessary one offering students the opportunity to become responsible citizens. More radical theorists such as Bowles and Gintis (1976) see the hidden curriculum as a way of preparing students to take their place in a socioeconomic system. They claim that middle and working-class students are socialized differentially, with the middle class involved in high levels of cognitive inputs, taught with flexibility, and given the opportunity for interpersonal development. For the working-class students, however, Bowles and Gintis claim that their relationship with the schooling process is marked by a high degree of certainty, control, and student powerlessness. There is explicitness in the criteria for student evaluation, rule following is enforced, and the hierarchy of authority is well defined. Students who do not acquiesce to official authority are made to suffer the consequences through low grades, negative evaluations, and a withdrawal of privileges. Working-class students dislike such explicit top-down policies and codes of conduct, so conflict, tension, and opposition abound between "rule makers" and "rule breakers."

Closely linked to the tensions and conflicts surrounding the routines of everyday school life is opposition to the formal curriculum. Research on tracking and the stratification of knowledge in American, British, and Canadian schools indicates that the working-class and racial minorities are more likely than their white, middle-class peers to be in low-track programs. It is such placement that determines minorities' future positions in the occupational hierarchy. Working-class and racial minority students have become very much aware of their futures and actively reject a curriculum that commits them to a future of generalized labor. Ogbu (1974) and Weis's (1985) explorations of black cultural forms in U.S. schools found that conflict with the school curriculum and lowered work efforts result when students realize that their education is only "second best" to that of whites. In her test of Bowles and Gintis's hypothesis that schools fragment students into tracks, then reward their capabilities, attitudes, and behaviors in different ways, Oakes (1985) concludes that the hidden and formal curriculum are inextricably related to each other and also to the broader socioeconomic system. Students with insights into how school structures limit their social advancement in life become antagonistic to such structures, making schools an arena for conflict. How does this struggle fit into the broader theoretical framework of schooling, social reproduction, and resistance? Let us now examine some of the theories that explain the culture-structure dualism.

The reproduction theorists such as Bourdieu and Passeron (1977) and Bowles and Gintis (1976) maintain that institutions such as schools perpetuate people's social-class positions in society. Bowles and Gintis, in particular, hypothesized that the capitalist economic system is a hierarchical structure that requires people of various social origin and educational preparation for its smooth operation. Schools are instrumental in educating, socializing, and delivering to the workplace people for these categories of work. To ensure that the social relationships of a stratified workplace are maintained, the school teaches respect for authority and the institutional hierarchy. This parallel between the social relationships of the school and the workplace is described by Bowles and Gintis as the "correspondence theory." How is education structured so that working and middle-class children are prepared differentially for their work roles? Here, Bowles and Gintis suggest that working-class children invariably are educated in neighborhood schools whose unwritten curriculum puts emphasis on subordinacy to authority, rule following and direction taking. This type of education, over time, reproduces generations of working-class and racial minorities at the bottom of the socioeconomic hierarchy with very little chance of upward mobility. Middle-class students, on the other hand, are educated in suburban schools that teach internalized control and give students the opportunity to participate in the decision-making process. This prepares them for more managerial positions in the stratified work force.

Giroux (1983) criticized the theory of social reproduction for being too deterministic. Students are not passive role-bearers or pawns in the capitalist system as Bowles and Gintis make them out to be; to the contrary, they exercise relative autonomy and actively resist the school structures they dislike.

Willis's (1977) research described a vibrant student culture that opposes and contests the regularities of schooling. His theory of cultural production labels the process by which subordinate groups such as his working-class, disenfranchized "lads" develop strident attitudes and practices in opposition to their kind of schooling. Is Willis's emphasis on the cultural also an extreme response to the uncritical structuralist explanation of schooling and social reproduction? Giroux's indepth analysis of the structure-culture dualism has provided a framework to examine these extreme accounts of schooling and the possibilities for bridging this dualism. He argues that the structuralist perspective is important because it identifies the economic, political,and ideological forces in society that shape the domination of the subordinate groups. With these structures in place, domination appears to "exhaust the possibility of struggle, resistance and transformation" (Giroux 1983:137).

The structuralists attach no significance to any form of contestation, struggle, and opposition to dominant institutional practices. The culturalists, on the other hand, insist on the relative autonomy of the cultural and the conscious struggle and actions of subordinate groups. But they fail to acknowledge the power of institutional mechanisms to control and shape human experiences. For example, Willis was aware of the structural determinants that shaped the attitudes and behaviors of the working-class "lads," but he did not analyze or elaborate on their full impact. For West Indian minorities in Canadian institutions, the imposition of dominant-group norms, values, social practices, and expectations on a group socialized in another culture has a significant impact on the content, process, and outcome of schooling. This study analyzes the structure-culture impact on school life as these forces strive to dominate each other.

THEORIES OF RESISTANCE AND CULTURAL INVERSION

Resistance theories developed out of studies that examine the opposition, confrontation ,and struggle between student cultures and the school's authority structure. But may all oppositional behaviors be defined as resistant? In developing his theory of resistance, Giroux (1983) insists that oppositional behaviors must have sociopolitical significance to be seen as resistance. When students refuse to follow certain school rules and routines and refuse to embrace school ethos that they perceive as acts of subordination, they are engaging in acts of resistance. When black students in Fordham and Ogbu's (1986) study rebuke their black peers for "acting white," they are actively resisting white structure and domination. Likewise, when black college students in Weis's (1985) study go through the routine of schooling but exert little effort in their study, they may be resisting an education that they see as only "second best" to that of whites. Dhondy's (1974:45) observation of rejection of school curriculum in British schools fits the definition of black culture of resistance:

> Their [blacks'] rejection of work is a rejection of the level to which schools have skilled them as a labor power, and when the community feeds that rejection back into the school system, it becomes a rejection of the function of schooling.

This negative response to the dominant-group prescription of education for the workplace fits Giroux's definition of resistance: the cause and meaning of opposition has "a great deal to do with moral and political indignation" (p.288). Giroux and others caution that not all oppositional behaviors of students have radical significance or are rooted in a reaction to authority. Hargreaves (1982) criticized researchers for their indiscriminate application of the category "resistance" to all student behaviors and using the concept as a sort of trawling device that does not distinguish between resistance and other modes of student responses. Mullard (1985) suggests that resistance should be seen as an expression of power relationships where socially distinct groups interact competitively, each possessing interests that are "anchored in diametrically alternative conception of social reality" (p.38). Student subcultures, then, use oppositional behaviors to dismantle the social and institutional structures of schools and replace them with ones that are more compatible with their own needs and desires.

What frame of reference is most appropriate for explaining forms of resistance practiced by immigrant minorities in a host society? Here, Ogbu's (1987) cultural differences and cultural inversion theories are useful starting points for analysing the behaviors of West Indian immigrant students. According to Ogbu, immigrant minorities possess a distinctive ethnic, linguistic,and cultural identity developed in their homeland before coming into contact with the host culture. West Indian immigrants to Britain or Punjabi immigrants to the U.S. demonstrate behaviors, language, and communication patterns that stand out as a part of their group's cultural and social identity. Secondary cultural differences, Ogbu explains, develop when two groups come into contact involving the subordination of one group. Such cultural differences are evident in what he describes as castelike minorities such as native, Mexican, and black Americans whose cultures have been subordinated by the dominant group over a long period of time. These secondary cultural differences are acts of resistance and opposition to the low status prescribed for them by the dominant culture. While primary cultural differences of immigrant groups are seen as one of content, secondary differences of castelike minorities are categorized as one of style. Studies of minorities in U.S. schools describe their differences from the dominant culture in terms of "communication style," "interaction style" and "behavior style." Minority groups have used these cultural styles very effectively in their practice of "cultural inversion." This Ogbu describes as the tendency for minorities to use their cultural style to resist dominant-group institutional practices, to protect and maintain their social identity, and to reject the negative stereotypes used to portray them.

This study of West Indian boys extends Ogbu's theory by examining how these immigrant students combine their primary and secondary cultural differences in a unique strategy of resistance to their school structures. Their content-style dualism has the potential to generate additional attitudes, symbols, and behaviors that are very dynamic in their oppositional practices. Some black students in the British school system embrace the Rastafarian subculture with its corresponding differences in language forms, dress, and demeanor and antiestablishment modes of behavior that are antithetical to dominant-group norms and values. This cultural inversion results in "the coexistence of two opposing cultural frames of reference..." (Ogbu 1987:323).

This brief overview of resistance theories will be helpful in putting into perspective the relationship that exists between the authority structure of Lumberville High School and the West Indian student subculture. Ogbu's theory of primary and secondary cultural differences has provided the framework for the study of minority group immigrants and their practice of cultural inversion to oppose institutional structures.

THE CANADIAN ENCOUNTER

Black West Indian culture and struggle is a novel feature of the Canadian classroom. This book delves into the lives of a group of black immigrant boys to show how they employ their cultural resources to resist those aspects of schooling that dominate their lives. But what implications does this culture of resistance have for the boys' social relations in school, and for the dominant-minority group dichotomy in the Canadian society at large? Do the boys themselves see race and color as a significant mediating factor in their interaction with dominant-group students, teachers, and school authority? Such evidence could call into question Wilson's (1978) claim of the declining significance of race in American, and in this case, Canadian society. How does the boys' culture of resistance restrict their educational opportunities that will, in turn, determine the place they take in the country's socioeconomic structure? If these black, working-class students accept the folk theory that education is the only way of "making it" in white society, why do they actively resist the school structure in which this valuable commodity may be received? How do they negotiate this delicate balance between accommodation to education and resistance to the structures that provide education?

It is an accepted fact that tracking and the stratification of knowledge prepare students for different stations in life. Have students at Lumberville penetrated this ideology and therefore reject the capacity of the school's formal curriculum to deliver the appropriate education for their social advancement in Canadian society? Students in other settings respond differently to schooling they perceive as leading nowhere. In this study we analyze potentially transformative endeavors of the boys to escape schooling that reproduces their low-class status in Canadian society. Driven by the achievement ideology, the students explore extracurricular sport as a viable alternative to the formal curriculum and explore intricate "escape routes" out of a school they perceive as a barrier to progress. Do they achieve their aspirations through these creative ventures or do the structural confines of schooling overcome human agency? An analysis of these powerful forces later in this book provides some answers to these questions.

The issues raised in this book are important in comparing Canada with other Western democracies in the schooling of racial minorities. Canada's policy on multiculturalism has led racial minority immigrants to expect an open opportunity structure with equal access to education and other life opportunities. But has the "black tile" in the Canadian cultural mosaic been afforded any better opportunities than racial minorities in countries such as the United States and Britain where expressed practices are to "melt the ethnics" and assimilate them culturally? These issues of policy and pedagogy are critical for educators contemplating multicultural and antiracist education for ethnically and racially diverse school populations. This account of a Canadian school encounter with a group of black immigrant students raises sensitive questions about structures and practices in multiracial classrooms. For example, does the racial culture now evident within schools compromise the pedagogical process? Are the oppositional responses of black students a result of too wide a gap between their achievement ideology and the opportunity structure?

To seek answers to these questions and to capture the interaction between a black student subculture and the school structure in which it operates, I utilized a qualitative research strategy. This approach provided an "inside perspective" of the conflict between black students and the authority structure of the school. Within this larger framework of qualitative methods the ethnographic approach proved ideal for portraying the social reality of the subculture in relation to the dominant school culture. For a one-and-a-half-year period starting in the spring of 1983, I immersed myself in the life of Lumberville High School. During this time I identified a cohesive group of black adolescent boys and documented their interactions and relationships with peers, teachers, and school administrators. Participant observation was conducted inside and outside classrooms and during extracurricular activities. These observations extended beyond the boundaries of the school and into the boys' neighborhoods and homes. The data gathering process was multimodal, employing individual and group interviews with focal students, teachers, coaches, administrators, and parents. Data from these sources were further supplemented and corroborated by secondary documentary data to give a holistic picture of the boys and the regularities of the school (See appendix A for a full description of the research methods).

The ethnography that emerged from such fieldwork reflects the range of behaviors, feelings, conflicts, and tensions expressed by marginalized students. Informants' perspectives were quite often in conflict with each other and also with the official position of the school. But such contradictory accounts of the schooling process are not unusual in such an arena of conflict. It was only by a variety of data collection methods that satisfactory levels of reliability and validity were achieved. Qualitative studies are not theory-free; researchers utilize theoretical assumptions to help them make sense of the data they accumulate. For this study, the paradigm shift from social and cultural reproduction theories to resistance theories provided the framework for explaining the social inequality generated by the process of schooling within my research setting. However, the inadequacy of these models as analytic tools opened the possibility for incorporating other theories.

In this introductory chapter, I have documented the rise in schools of oppositional cultures mediated by social class, gender, and more specifically, race. With emphasis on racial forms of culture, a comparative overview of black oppositional cultures in the U.S., British, and now Canadian schools was presented along with the theoretical perspectives postulated for such opposition to school structures. In chapter 2, black life and schooling in Canadian society will be placed in an historical perspective, comparing the pre-twentieth-century era with post-1967 West Indian immigrant life in Canada, "the land of opportunity." This historical overview provides a backdrop for a detailed study of black cultural forms in a Canadian high school today. Chapters 3 through 5 are mainly descriptive, detailing black students' creation of an oppositional social identity, while chapter 6 explains how school structures contribute to this culture. In these chapters I supplement the traditional ethnography with related literature highlighting the similarities and differences among black oppositional styles in different multiracial societies. Chapter 7 analyzes the outcomes of the spiralling interaction between school structure and student cultures. These outcomes are put in the context of the students' projected position within Canada's socioeconomic structure. Chapter 8 suggests strategies for reducing black oppositional forms and increasing the educational opportunities of black, working-class students in Canadian schools.

CHAPTER 2

Black Life and Schooling in Canada

During the nineteenth and twentieth centuries, Canada was perceived as the land of refuge and opportunity for two separate groups of blacks. The first were blacks fleeing slavery in the United States and seeking refuge in Canada. The second were West Indians leaving behind them postcolonial depression and limited opportunities, and arriving in Canada seeking socioeconomic advancement. Both groups provided Canada with the much-needed labor power for frontier building in the nineteenth century and economic expansion in the post-World War II era of the twentieth century.

This chapter provides a brief overview of the first group of black Canadians as they strove to participate in the country's economic, social, and educational institutions. A more extensive account is provided of the second group, West Indian immigrants, as they struggled for employment equity for themselves and educational opportunities for their children. More specifically, this chapter zeroes in on an urban, working-class community of West Indian immigrants, examines their cultural responses to the opportunity structure, and analyzes the schooling available to their children. Where is the schooling of this particular group of immigrant children preparing them to fit in Canada's occupational hierarchy? How does this new group of blacks differ from the old in defining itself in relation to the dominant white culture? Let us now explore these themes.

BLACK LIFE BEFORE THE WEST INDIANS

The history of black life in Canada goes back to 1632 with the first record of Negro slaves in New France (Quebec). Winks's (1971) comprehensive history of blacks in Canada describes the utility of slaves in this French colony as rarely extending beyond domestic use since its economy did not require their large-scale use comparable to that of the sugar and cotton economies of the

17

West Indies and the Southern United States. The status of slaves, their use, and their relationship with their owners were regulated by French laws and monitored by the Catholic church. Under the British, Walker (1985) documents, the population of blacks increased sharply with the arrival of black Loyalists from the U.S. They won their freedom by fighting on the behalf of the British during the American Revolutionary War. During the War of 1812 between the Americans and Canada, thousands of black slaves fled slavery in the U.S. and were not only offered sanctuary in Canada, but were promised free land in Nova Scotia and New Brunswick.

The blacks that entered Canada alongside whites as British Empire Loyalists were quickly disappointed when they were accorded differential treatment. They often waited longer than whites for their allotment of land and were put to work on such projects as repairing barracks. When they eventually received land, their allotments were substantially smaller than what was promised, were in poor locations, and rocky in quality. Winks documents the gradual straining of the relationship between black and white settlers in the Nova Scotia area as both groups competed for good land and scarce job opportunities. Black communities became alienated from the white's and within the black group itself; black Loyalist settlers behaved in a superior fashion to the enslaved. In the province of Ontario, fugitive slaves from the U.S. gradually increased the number of blacks who were welcomed as labor to clear the land and construct roads. The Fugitive Slave Act of 1850 saw the growth of Ontario's black population and the Underground Railroad flourished during this era, delivering black American slaves to freedom in Canada, "The Promised Land."

After the Canadian Confederation in 1867, American blacks were attracted by recruitment campaigns to Canada's prairie provinces of Alberta, Saskatchewan, and Manitoba to settle as farmers. However, a public campaign to curtail the entry of black settlers from the U.S. spearheaded the propaganda that Negroes who had taken land in Canada had not proved themselves satisfactory as farmers, thrifty as settlers, or desirable (as) neighbors (Winks 1971:309). Such campaigns urged government officials to "preserve for the sons of Canada the land they proposed to give to niggers" (p.309). Driven by such antiblack sentiments, Canadian immigration officials launched a campaign in the U.S., discouraging black settlers from coming to Canada on the grounds that there was racial prejudice, and, furthermore, the Canadian climatic conditions were too severe for them to survive. Such a policy of persuasion was further bolstered by rigid restrictions at border points that refused the entry of blacks on grounds of health, literacy, and financial support. By 1912, Troper (1972) writes, the number of blacks entering Canada was reduced to a few while the rejections, presumably many blacks, rose significantly. This was followed by black return migration to the U.S. The only other wave of black immigration to Canada of note was that from California to Vancouver Island during the 1850s when hundreds of blacks settled in Victoria and were employed in business enterprises there. Winks (1971:313) documents that when criticized for its selective and racist immigration practices, the Canadian government's response was that:

> The Dominion government retained the power to prohibit entry "to any nationality or race" if "such immigrants are deemed undesirable having regard to the climatic, industrial, social, educational, labor or other conditions" of Canada or "because of other probable inability to become readily assimilated."

Did blacks experience the freedom, equality, and full participation in Canadian life over the years? Historians such as Winks (1971) and Walker (1985) document that, from the outset, blacks who entered whether as Loyalists in the East, fugitives in Ontario, farmers in the prairies or business entrepreneurs on Vancouver Island, were socially and physically isolated from whites and were treated as "subordinates' with low status and incomplete citizenship. Walker (1985:9) describes their position within Canadian society:

> Marginal, segregated and dependent, the free black group constituted a distinct caste which ranked beneath the lowest whites. Occupational and residential exclusivity was matched in the churches and schools, where blacks were segregated or excluded.

Across Canada, Walker documents, blacks were denied equality: churches established segregated sections for black worshippers, some public facilities refused them service, and theatres relegated them to balcony seats. Any efforts on the part of blacks to break the color line would result in white hostility, public petitions, tighter restrictions, and further alienation.

This exclusionary and alienating behavior of white against black Canadians was also evident in time of national crisis. During World War I, patriotic blacks were systematically excluded from serving their country alongside their white compatriots. However, as the war dragged on and manpower became scarce, Winks (1971:318) writes, blacks were trained for labor battalions because of "their great capacity for manual work" and sent to Europe to serve in the Canadian Forestry Corps, logging, milling, and shipping until the end of the war. Fostering the white treatment of blacks in Canada was the racist ideology that justified the Negro's inferior position in society. They were often stereotyped in early twentieth-century Canadian publications as slow-witted, lazy, superstitious, inferior and disruptive, sexually aggressive with animal appetites. Scientific racism supported this ideology postulating the theory that the genetic superiority of Europeans was responsible for their achievements and the colonization of peoples with darker skin. Restrictions on black immigration to Canada were partly based on the myth that the Aryan races would not wholesomely amalgamate with Africans and Asiatics;

this would result in a "mongrel race." These restrictions continued until the late 1960s.

BLACK SCHOOLING

The schooling of blacks in Canada's history followed the pattern of segregation experienced in other social institutions. In Winks's account, education for blacks in the early stages was organized by the church that provided an alternative to the public school system. The intensity of the prejudice directed toward black children during nineteenth-century Canada made it impossible for them to achieve equality of educational opportunity. For example, Winks (1971:364) viewed black education in Nova Scotia as "mechanical, rooted in an increasingly outgrown curriculum, badly taught in unattractive buildings by only semi-literate teachers...." This situation persisted across Canada and was intensely debated in Ontario where whites worked unceasingly to remove black children from the public schools. While school districts denied black admission to their schools, they actively petitioned the provincial government to create separate school facilities for blacks.

In 1849, the Negro Separate School legislation was passed giving school boards the legal authority to establish alternate schooling for blacks wherever the need arose. Again, the quality of education in these schools fell below the standards of the public schools; there were no libraries, teacher competence was low, and the school year was shortened. During this period the church became instrumental in providing schooling for black students in many localities. Debate waged over the wisdom of creating a segregated school system and Egerton Ryerson, the Provincial School Superintendent responsible for pioneering this legislation,was denounced by opponents for encouraging "caste schools." Gradually, toward the end of the nineteenth century, the separate schools in Ontario were used less and less, and by 1917, the last remaining were closed. It was not until 1964, however, that this Separate School legislation was officially repealed.

From this overview of black life, historians such as Winks have painted the picture of a racial group subordinated by whites and alienated from the mainstream. Blacks were not only alienated from the dominant group, but from each other. First, they were fragmented into regional pockets from Nova Scotia in the east to British Columbia in the west with very few linkages that would help in the building of a black national identity. Second, black ethnicity and social class became divisive forces as such groups as the old-line loyalists flaunted superiority to fugitive-line blacks or descendants of the Jamaican Maroons. Winks (1971:477) characterized the Canadian black as "divided, withdrawn [and] without a substantial body of shared historical experience" or a "national heritage to fall back on for self-identification." It is against this historical backdrop of black life and schooling in Canada that a new, somewhat more cohesive group of blacks arrived from the West Indies, with a shared historical experience, a common cultural heritage, a concentrated resettlement pattern in the host society and with the potential to challenge more effectively the established racial order.

ENTER THE WEST INDIANS

Prior to the 1960s there was no established route for large-scale West Indian immigration to Canada.[1] The "Domestic Scheme" of the 1950s and 1960s gave young West Indian women the opportunity to work in Canada as domestic servants. These women worked in households in seventeen cities across Canada, making it difficult for them to maintain any group identity. After the one-year domestic service requirement, many established themselves in other careers such as nursing, or moved to the U.S. to pursue other interests. The only other group of West Indians in Canada were students at universities scattered across the country. They also were alienated from dominant-group Canadians and maintained their social distance in campus life. Off campus they did not establish relationships with the less-educated black community in Halifax, Nova Scotia, nor the "domestic" in Montreal and other cities. According to Henry (1968), both the domestics and the students led a self-contained social life and relied on their own internal networking for social sustenance. From the outset, then, these two small groups of West Indians in Canada forged separate identities because of their alienation from the mainstream culture and social-class differentiation between each other. These two factors would also be instrumental in the identity formation of future West Indian immigrants to arrive in Canada.

During the 1960s a number of "pull" factors combined to increase the flow of West Indian immigrants to Canada. Pressure was put on Canada by "Third World" nations to reverse its discriminatory immigration policies that rejected immigrants by reason of race, national origins, religion, and sex. These pressures, combined with the demand for immigrant labor to meet Canada's expanding postwar economy needs and the need for Third World markets to sell their products, forced Canada to expand immigration along nondiscriminatory lines. The opening of immigration offices in West Indian countries such as Jamaica, Trinidad, Barbados, and Guyana facilitated the application and screening of prospective immigrants to Canada. New regulations in 1962 made education, skills, and training the main conditions of admissibility; and in 1967, they were amended to introduce the "points system" (see appendix B). In this, specific value or "points" were assigned to characteristics such as education, language, age, personal suitability, and employment prospects. By the 1970s, the West Indies jumped from fourteenth to third as the source of Canada's immigrants, with the West Indian newcomers settling almost exclusively in urban areas, Montreal and Toronto being the most popular destinations.

WEST INDIANS IN TORONTO

West Indians measure their success in Canada by comparing their achievements with their primary motivation for migration: economic and social mobility. How successful are West Indians living in Toronto in achieving the desired employment and income, housing accommodation, and education advancement for their children?

Ramcharan's (1976) research probed the extent to which the skills, knowledge, and educational training of West Indian immigrants are utilized in the quest to fulfil their economic aspirations and expectations in Canada. From this analysis factors such as occupational status and length of residence in Canada appeared to be the major explanatory variables affecting the economic adaptation of West Indian immigrants in Toronto. For example, Ramcharan (1976:298) states:

> Thirty-three percent of white collar workers were unable to obtain jobs of the same status as in their former country. However, the most severe initial status loss occurred for blue collar workers.... Only 26% of these workers found suitably commensurate jobs, with the majority having to accept jobs as unskilled or service workers.

Henry and Ginsberg's (1985) study of racial minorities' entry into the job market revealed substantial barriers; racial discrimination in employment can occur at all levels of employer-employee and applicant interaction. By systematically researching the experiences of whites relative to nonwhites in their job search efforts, differential treatment by employers was revealed. The researchers found that blacks' chances of receiving a job offer are only one out of twenty, while whites' chances are three of every twenty. Henry and Ginsberg (1985:5) conclude: "There is a clear preference by a large proportion of Toronto employers for white employees."

Gatekeeping by employers and their denial of equal access of employment to nonwhite applicants have put the West Indian at a serious disadvantage in the labor market. After entry into the labor market, socioeconomic indicators such as income levels, occupational status, and underrepresentation in senior management positions point to a confined inequality of blacks. Abella's (1984) analysis of the 1981 census data revealed that:

> Black (immigrant) males, especially those arriving after 1970 seem to have a lower economic level than other males, and the disparity between the income of Caribbean males and the national average for all males was 11%.

When such factors as education, knowledge of English, and work experience were controlled, black men and women in Toronto earned significantly
less than other ethnic group members. Goldlust and Richmond's (1973) analysis of the 1971 census data found that blacks and Asians earned nearly $3,000
less than other immigrant groups. Similarly, a decade later, an Ontario Human
Rights Commission Report (1983) on the experience of visible minorities in
the work force found that Masters of Business Administration (M.B.A.) graduates who were members of a visible minority group earned, on the average,
$3,000 less than their white counterparts. In higher status occupations, black
professionals earned less than their white counterparts. These significant findings point to the fact that income inequality is evident at all levels of employment. Henry and Ginsberg (1985:14) conclude: "Employment has profound
effects on the quality of life that members of a racial minority group can obtain
and these effects are both cumulative and intergenerational."

In the area of living accommodation, during the early to mid-1970s,
Head and Lee (1975) found that over sixty percent of West Indians surveyed
in Toronto perceived that they had experienced housing discrimination.
Walker (1984) concludes that since darker-skinned West Indians reported
three times the number of cases as fairer-skinned "brown" West Indians, and
over ten times the number reported by white immigrants, such discrimination
was racially motivated.

Black integration into community life was further delayed by incidents of
racial violence against them in public places. Studies such as Adair and Rosenstock (1976; 1977) reported an increase in racial slurs, insults, and assaults on
black children on school grounds, while the Ontario Human Rights Commission (1977) and Head and Lee (1975) reported unwarranted harassment of
blacks by the police. Moreover, there is the perception among West Indians
that the police often stereotype blacks as law breakers, and are more inclined to
be zealous in investigating and charging them, even with minor offenses.

West Indians' perceptions of racial discrimination are validated by white
Canadians themselves who identified this and other nonwhite groups as the
most frequent victims of discrimination. According to Walker (1984), in
1981, seventy-nine percent named West Indians as victims, a figure almost
identical to the West Indians' own perceptions. On "acceptability scales" and
"social standing lists," blacks continue to be rated one of the least accepted
by dominant-group white Canadians. From this general situation Walker
(1984:19) concludes:

> Awareness of this general situation combined frequently with personal
> experience of discrimination, damages the fulfilment of West Indian expec-
> tations and their integration into Canadian society.

As a response to their social isolation from dominant-group white Canadians, West Indians have formed cultural, religious, athletic, and political

activist organizations for mutual support. Despite the problems of adaptation, West Indians' satisfaction with the move to Canada appears to increase with the length of residence in Canada. There is faith among West Indians that they will ultimately achieve occupational mobility.

WEST INDIAN CHILDREN IN TORONTO SCHOOLS

Following the post-1967 influx of West Indian immigrants into the metropolitan Toronto area, it became evident that their children were faltering within the school system. From some impressionistic and empirical studies such as Wright's (1970), Roth's (1974), and Barret's (1980) emerged some salient concerns about their schooling. West Indian students were underachieving academically; their performance was affected negatively by perceived discrimination; and there was an emerging subculture that was in conflict with the authority structure of the school.

Working-class West Indian immigrant parents and their children perceive education as the only mobility channel open to them in Canada. As a result, they place very high value on education and rank it most important to them, above family, happiness, love, freedom, jobs, and money. Calliste's (1982) research also shows that West Indians, when compared with other ethnic groups such as South Europeans and Anglo-Canadians, were more likely to have higher educational and occupational expectations. She argues that the higher educational expectations of working-class West Indians may mean that "they are more highly motivated, more achievement-oriented, and more likely to expect to be upwardly mobile than working-class Anglo-Canadians" (p.17). How do these high expectations translate into program placement?

Wright and Tsuji (1984) found that West Indian students were represented in all levels of high school programs, from low-level vocational to high-level university oriented programs. However, data collected routinely by the Toronto Board of Education since 1970 showed that blacks and native Canadians have the highest representation in the low-level vocational and occupational programs and the lowest representation in high-level university oriented programs. Working-class West Indian parents express disillusionment that their children were diverted away from programs that would lead to higher-status white collar jobs. Instead, they were being channelled into vocational and technical programs that connote status immobility and academic failure.

Some researchers are convinced that the most difficult problem faced by black students in the Toronto school system is related to race and color. Ramcharan's (1975) survey of West Indian parents and their children in the school system revealed a high percent of complaints about racial discrimination practiced by white classmates and teachers. Ijaz's (1980:180) findings also support the belief that white Canadian children often have highly negative attitudes towards blacks, Indians and Pakistani:

> The values and attitudes cherished by white Canadian children are largely characterized by profound feelings of prejudice toward other ethnic groups, particularly toward the colored minority groups.

What is the impact of racism on the black child in school? A psychiatrist, daCosta (1978:7), criticized the school environment as "the arena in which these (racial minority) children first experience sustained intolerance and denigration by their peers." Not only does racial discrimination cause social relationships between whites and nonwhites to deteriorate, but "the nonwhite child becomes a product of a system that is seen as causing irreparable psychological scars" (p.7).

WEST INDIAN SUBCULTURES IN TORONTO SCHOOLS

The emergence of West Indian youth subcultures in Metro Toronto schools may be perceived as opposition to school structures and the antagonistic relationship forged with the dominant group of students within the school and the community. Anderson and Grant's (1975) survey of West Indian children's adjustment in Metro Toronto schools revealed contradictory yet useful data on student-teacher relationships. For example, the practice of clique formation among West Indian high school students was perceived by teachers as "ganging up," and the association of such group formation with "black power" (p. 153). Perceived discomfort on the part of their teachers made these students more overt in their protest, utilizing even more subcultural behaviors. Anderson and Grant (1975:153) describe some of these activities, and the reaction they evoked:

> They [West Indian students] admit to skipping classes sometimes, but claim that on most occasions they are merely pursuing ethnic or culturally based activities which do not conflict with the school timetable, for example, playing "soul" music after school. They also perceive certain types of dress, popular among them, as a source of irritation to the school administration. School personnel have been reluctant or refused outright to permit the formation of black-based cultural clubs or associations.

Culture-based group formation and the leadership stance taken by black students were interpreted by school staff as a "militant posture." Although daCosta (1978) saw these responses as part of the adolescent's emancipatory behavior, and a way of defining self and racial components of student identity, "the adaptive function of these behaviors can be invalidated if they are seen as pathological behaviors" (p.6).

The conceptualization of black cultural forms within Toronto schools as deviant or pathological had become the teacher's paradigm. This perspective closely paralleled that of British educators who utilize notions of cultural deprivation and family pathology as the primary explanations for student disaffection. From these studies one may conclude that educators' beliefs in the impact of adverse family and cultural factors limit their interpretation of counterschool behaviors.

To summarize, the literature on working-class West Indians in Toronto characterizes them as immigrants striving for socioeconomic mobility in a society that tends to restrict particular ethnic and racial minorities. As Tepperman (1975:142) points out, "If there is little mobility after arrival particular ethnic groups tend to preserve their 'entrance status' for decades and perhaps generations after entering Canada."

The emergence of black youth subcultures such as the ones described by Anderson and Grant may be a response to the curriculum content, the authority structure, and the intergroup relations they experience in school. Such a response takes on an identity that differentiates itself from dominant group norms, values, and life-styles; dress style, activities that oppose school rules, and a "militant posture" are some of the behaviors that characterize black identity formation. This new black cultural response to schooling differs qualitatively from that of earlier blacks in Canada, and carries emancipatory possibilities from subordination.

Student cultures are informed by the wider community in which they are located. Communities have to be seen then as not merely organic, but also political entities in which people struggle to develop and maintain a sought-after life-style. The Lumber Valley North community described in the next section is texturized within class and ethnicity and exerts tremendous influence on the culture of the students who reside within it.

THE COMMUNITY AND THE SCHOOL

The Lumber Valley North community (a pseudonym) is located on the periphery of metropolitan Toronto, and experienced rapid development and population growth in the recent past. One of the most dramatic changes in the Lumber Valley North district is the rapid diversification of its language and ethnic makeup. Census Canada (1981) reports that from 1976 to 1981, residents with a mother tongue other than English or French, Canada's official languages, increased by fifty-four percent, the largest of these groups being Italians. Notwithstanding, mother tongue affiliation is not a good indicator of ethnocultural group membership since most West Indians report English as their mother tongue, but adhere to their own cultural background in other respects.

The rapid population change of the community brought about an increase in social problems. High-density development changed the physical and social structure of the community, as high-rise housing and government-subsidized accommodation threw residents close together. Unemployment was relatively high, with the fifteen to twenty-four year age group suffering the greatest handicap because of a low job concentration ratio and inadequate transportation services. The community organizations serving the area identified inadequate training in schools and irrelevant job skills as factors contributing to youth unemployment.

The family structure within the community underwent significant changes. There has been an increase in lone-parent families; about thirteen percent of the families were headed by one parent. The widowed or divorced population has shown an increase of forty-four percent between 1976 and 1981 (Census Canada 1981). Social conditions gave rise to crime and juvenile delinquency in the Lumber Valley North community; teenagers were involved in vandalism, drinking, and loitering around plazas, parks, and apartment stairwells. On any given day, groups of teenagers can be seen "hanging out" on street corners. The situation is even more acute in some high-density neighborhoods. A parent of a student in this study complained about the unsafe social conditions in her neighborhood:

> To me it's a jungle down here. I have told my children, "Always keep your back to the wall and then you can protect your front." There are a few kids they hang around with that I don't like, but I would say that my kids are one hundred percent educated to survive on the streets. Some days I come home and there are lots of kids around, ten to twelve of them older ones from eighteen to twenty-five years old.

Students as well as staff at Lumberville refer to the Jones Park neighborhood (located near the school) as "the ghetto" or "the dump, where welfare cases come from." A student confided:

> I wouldn't live in that place (Jones Park). I don't mix up with those kind of people, they are crooked...around there is messy; you see windows broken. They paint all kinds of things on the walls.

Racial tension, mostly between whites and blacks, and even incidents of racial violence have flared in such neighborhoods where a diversity of racial and cultural groups is highly concentrated. The police, the court system, and correctional services have all reported an increase in the number of cases they deal with from this community.

The socioeconomic problems of the Lumber Valley North community, and more specifically, the Jones Park neighborhood adjacent to Lumberville High include high unemployment, low-income subsidized housing, high juvenile delinquency and crime rates, and a constant turnover in population. It is from this changing, working-class community that most of Lumberville's students come, thus creating the type of working-class school atmosphere, program, and students I describe in the next section.

LUMBERVILLE HIGH: ITS PROGRAMS AND STUDENTS

Lumberville High offers the lowest-level academic program of the school district's multilevel high school system (see figure 1). Its relatively small student population of approximately 355 with a staff complement of thirty-four, has experienced a gradual declining enrollment from a high of approximately 450 students in the 1970s. The school, opened in the mid-1960s, is a result of a plan where the federal government worked cooperatively with provincial and municipal governments throughout Canada in developing trade schools, vocational schools, and the vocational components of composite high schools. The objective of Lumberville then was to prepare students not intending to pursue postsecondary education, for reasons of lower ability or lack of interest, for entry into employment. The goals of the Lumberville program were threefold: a) to enable students to learn occupational skills in a secondary school setting; b) to develop the self-image of the students by providing an environment where success is more readily attained; c) to enable the student to feel comfortable in group enterprise.

FIGURE 1
Structure of Lumber Valley School District Programs*

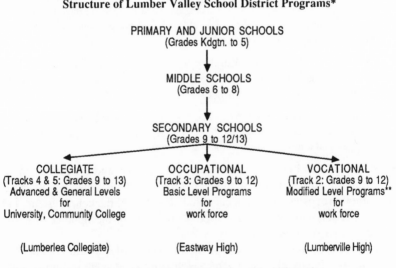

PRIMARY AND JUNIOR SCHOOLS
(Grades Kdgtn. to 5)

MIDDLE SCHOOLS
(Grades 6 to 8)

SECONDARY SCHOOLS
(Grades 9 to 12/13)

COLLEGIATE	OCCUPATIONAL	VOCATIONAL
(Tracks 4 & 5: Grades 9 to 13)	(Track 3: Grades 9 to 12)	(Track 2: Grades 9 to 12)
Advanced & General Levels	Basic Level Programs	Modified Level Programs**
for	for	for
University, Community College	work force	work force
(Lumberlea Collegiate)	(Eastway High)	(Lumberville High)

Some elementary schools accommodate primary, junior, and middle grades.
*All names of schools and school districts are pseudonyms.
**This Modified Level designation was eliminated from use in the Ontario Ministry of Education circular, Ontario Schools: Intermediate and Senior Divisions (OSIS) 1984.

Admission Criteria:

Lumberville High School admits students who have an I.Q. of less than 90
and/or have attained less than a grade 6 level of achievement in reading,
mathematics, language and spelling.... Entering students must be 13 years
of age as of December 31st of their first year at the vocational school.

In 1984, the Ontario Ministry of Education eliminated the "vocational"
program designation with the introduction of new guidelines for Ontario
schools intermediate and secondary (O.S.I.S.). Many school districts around
the province reclassified their modified level program as basic, and have
offered to their students a two-tier program that they describe as "high basic"
and "low basic."

The teaching staff of Lumberville is predominantly white with an average teaching experience of over fifteen years. Harvey's (1980) survey found
the group equipped with a variety of educational and professional qualifications ranging from master's and bachelor's degrees in Education to specialist
certificates for teaching both academic and vocational subjects. While the
core of the staff was stable with the average length of over ten years at Lumberville and a turnover rate of about fifteen percent, the concern was
expressed among these teachers that their contract arrangements in a declining student population lent itself to the domino effect of "bumping."[2] Harvey
(1980:129) documents the views expressed by some of the teachers:

Teachers who enter the occupational and vocational programs in this way
often lack the skills and motivation to deal effectively with the needs of students in the occupational and vocational programs.

The program structure at Lumberville offers students a balance of academic and shop programs. From grade nine through twelve students spend
half their class time taking academic subjects and half in shop courses. The
academic courses listed in the selection guide include English, mathematics,
science, geography, history, law, physical and health education, media, and
introduction to computer studies. Vocational courses include: art, automotive
servicing, custodial services, cosmetology, drafting, electricity, food preparation, home economics, machine shop, merchandising, sewing and tailoring,
sheet metal, small engines, typing, and woodworking. Students in their first
year are exposed to a wide variety of shops, but in their last two years at Lumberville, their shop options are reduced to a major and a minor subject area.
Supplementing classroom courses are such programs as work experience and
cooperative education designed to help students "(b)ridge the gap between
theory taught in school and the potential applications expected in professional
commercial and industrial settings" (Course Selection Guide 1985:12).

Curriculum offerings are rather limited at the higher grades. Students
who exhaust these offerings are forced to consider a transfer to other high

schools with a wider selection of courses. In addition, fractional offerings of some course credits tend to prolong students' stay at Lumberville as this student points out:

> Ike: This year they give only half a credit in History. That means I have to
> attend for two years to get a full credit.

The credentials students receive at Lumberville vary with the years of schooling satisfactorily completed. A Certificate of Training is awarded to students who have reached a satisfactory level of skill development in a particular field by the end of their second year. At the 1983 and 1984 annual commencements, seventy-six and forty-seven students respectively were awarded the Certificate of Training. At the successful completion of the Lumberville school program, students receive the Ontario Secondary School Graduation Diploma. Twelve and fourteen students received this diploma in 1983 and 1984 respectively. Transcripts accompanying these diplomas indicate to prospective employers the level of difficulty (academic track) at which these programs were completed.

Lumberville's student population is unique in its ethnoracial and immigrant composition, its academic level of functioning, and in the socioeconomic status of its parents. The school has a large immigrant population. Harvey (1980:33) found that "one-third of the students were born outside Canada, the majority of these (25.6 percent) being from West Indian countries." In addition to West Indian immigrant children, the student body reflects the changing ethnic population of the Lumber Valley North community. There is a growing number of Indo-Pakistani and South Asian students. Students entering the school are usually younger than those of other secondary schools. The rationale given for this earlier transfer from middle schools was their difficulty with academic work.

Within the larger occupational structure, the parents of Lumberville students are primarily in the sales and service industries, processing, and other related industrial occupations. Harvey's data show that only a small number (8.3 percent) of students' fathers are in the managerial, administrative, and related professions and a large percent of mothers (25 percent) are unemployed, while a smaller percent (3 percent) was not in the labor force.

The employment patterns of past students of Lumberville reveal marked similarities with those of their parents. The rate of unemployment is high (37.5 percent had not held any jobs since completion of school), and those who have found jobs were likely to be in service or industrial occupations of processing and fabricating (Harvey 1980). These jobs are ranked in the lower cluster of occupations on the Pineo and Porter (1967) Canadian occupational prestige scale. Harvey's research confirms no intergenerational mobility in occupation; students entering the labor markets are starting at the same low level as their parents.

To summarize, this chapter provides an overview of the community life and schooling of two separate and distinct groups of blacks in Canada, one in the nineteenth, the other in the twentieth century. Despite the difference in time the comparison shows striking similarities in their low status in Canada's socioeconomic hierarchy and their alienated and subordinate social relationship with the dominant group. The twentieth-century blacks of West Indian origin, however, responded to their unequal status with a form of concerted, cultural resistance, somewhat different from that of black Canadians before them. The emergence of subcultures as formidable forces against the institutional structures has contributed in some way to the conflict and discomfort between dominant-group whites and subordinate blacks. Finally, we focused on the community where the socioeconomic conditions influence the structure of relationships among various racial and immigrant groups. It is from such a community that Lumberville students come. The next chapter focuses on the culture of one student group.

CHAPTER 3

The Jocks at Lumberville

Students' lived culture in school is not only influenced by their orientation toward the rules and regularities of the school, but also by the type of identity they are striving to create within the school and in the wider community. This chapter describes the subcultural lives of the Jocks: their group formation and interaction style, their language and communicative patterns, and their dress code and demeanor. Here I articulate how these students resort to, and elaborate on, cultural forms from their West Indian heritage as a response to the authority structure of the school. An analysis of such an identity formation process shows the potential for such oppositional attitudes and behaviors to separate the Jocks from the mainstream culture.

GROUP FORMATION AND MEMBERSHIP

A salient feature of student life at Lumberville High is its informal peer group formation based on the dynamics of racial background and ethnic identity. The Jocks, a black clique of high-profile senior boys, are all rooted in a West Indian ancestry and culture. Almost all are recent immigrants, raised in Jamaica until the time of migration to Canada. At Lumberville the Jocks belong to an informal network of sport enthusiasts starting with a small nucleus and expanding to other peripheral members such as teammates, classmates, and neighborhood buddies. Such a network extends to other schools as clique members who leave Lumberville for "greener pastures" maintain active contact with the Jocks. At the core are eight boys: Weston, Earl, Mitch, Ike, Roy, Byron, Boyd, and Leroy. Weston stands out in the group because he is the tallest. His six-foot height gives him a distinct advantage in games such as basketball. He projects himself as a model athlete, representing Lumberville in major sport competitions, and has won several athletic awards. Weston's gregarious personality incites his colleagues into pro as well as counter school activities. On the basketball court he motivates his teammates; in the back halls and corridors of the school he challenges his friends to break school rules. He sees some of his teachers as power-wielding authority figures controlling the lives of students. Weston's early life in Jamaica has equipped him with the dialect skills and other cultural competencies that enable him to interact with his friends entirely in that ethnocultural mode. For academic instruction, Weston is tracked to the middle group of the school's three-tiered grouping system for language instruction purposes.

Earl is the oldest member of the Jocks and exerts considerable influence on the group. He is the acknowledged leader and often shouts instructions and directions to his teammates in the heat of sport competitions. He is a fiery, quick-tempered lad who rises to the defense of his teammates in times of altercations with the opposition on the playing field as well as in the classroom. Earl's early life in rural Jamaica, his limited schooling there, and his resort to the vernacular for self-expression have earned him the nickname "Country." He uses the dialect unceasingly both in and out of class, and especially as an oppositional response to teachers who "bug" him. Academically, Earl is assessed as low functioning; part-time work cuts into his class time. He is in his final year of schooling before joining the work force on a full-time basis.

Mitch is quite the opposite of Earl in personality and style of behavior. Born in England of Jamaican parentage, he migrated to Canada with his mother and siblings at an early age. He is now eighteen years old and identifies completely with the Jamaican subculture. For example, he communicates well in both standard English and Jamaican dialect and engages in code-switching to suit the occasion. Mitch is "appearance-conscious" and works ceaselessly on "being cool" in his dress, language, and behavior. Both Mitch's older sister and brother, however, identify more with the mainstream culture at school, in the community, and at college. The majority of their friends are white and from the dominant culture, while Mitch's are black and from the West Indian subculture. This differential commitment to subcultural identity has been a source of concern for his mother since it affects, in a negative way, sibling relationships within the home. Mitch often speaks disparagingly of his siblings' "honky" friends. In school he is a dedicated athlete and has represented the school in volleyball, soccer, basketball, and track-and-field athletics. Mitch is popular with the student body at large and was elected to the presidency of the Student Council. However, espousing values defined in opposition to the dominant culture caused him to fall into serious conflicts with the school authorities resulting in his resignation from this student-elected position. Furthermore, his demotion from the top language class became a source of contention since such a move seriously jeopardized his much sought-after promotion to a higher-track school.

Ike is very popular among the Jocks and well respected within the school community. His popularity makes his home the gathering point for his friends after school and on weekends. Ike does not openly oppose school rules but among his friends he complains about the shortcomings of sports and academic programs at Lumberville. He is a dedicated athlete and contributes to the school's athletic programs both as a player and as an official in intramural games. Such demonstration of good citizenship has earned him several awards as well as respect from students and teachers alike. Ike is tracked to the middle stream for language instruction, but would rather be at a higher-level school with better sport programs. His mother supports such a transfer but for occupational rather than athletic opportunities.

Roy is a talkative, articulate Jock and is tracked to the top language group for academic instruction. Although he has the academic skills to function in a higher-track school, Roy is ambivalent about pursuing such a placement. He is of mixed race parentage and is the only Canadian-born student in the clique. He identifies very strongly with the West Indian subculture and has acquired the cultural competencies to operate within the group. Teachers perceive his association with the Jocks as that of a "hanger-on" for prestige and recognition within the social system of the school. In the sport arena he performs with flair, but his skill level is decidedly below that of his teammates. Roy has secured a place on school teams more so from association than by talent. He displays a rather superior attitude towards female students and threatens to "pound them out" if they get in his way. Byron is a graceful, talented athlete who leads by doing. He is well respected and liked by teachers, but maintains a close allegiance to his subcultural clique. He is a senior nearing graduation and finds it difficult to participate in extracurricular sport activities because of part-time job commitments.

Boyd, on the other hand, is quite often at odds with the school's authority structure and policies. His open defiance of school rules has brought him into several encounters with the law both at school and within the community. Boyd's frequent struggles with the school administration precipitated his departure from Lumberville in search of a school environment that is more compatible with his needs. However, he maintains regular contact with the Jocks by visiting their homes and attending athletic competitions in which his friends participate. Boyd's influence lies in lobbying for social change within Lumberville and persuading the Jocks to transfer to "better" schools if such changes are not forthcoming.

Leroy attends many academic and shop classes with the group, participates in team sports with the Jocks, lives in the same neighborhood, but is not readily embraced by the clique because of what they describe as his "laziness and low motivation in sport." He misses early morning training sessions and after-school team practices. He is a "minimum effort athlete" who makes school teams on the reputation of his friends. However, he identifies strongly with the group culture and contributes to subcultural activities that require such competencies as ethnospecific language and communication patterns, dress code, and behavior styles. Leroy reacts negatively to the school's authority structure and shows disdain for coaches who suspend him from teams.

Although the Jocks are assigned to different classes for language instruction, most of them choose or are assigned the same shop options and spend half the school day together. However, it is their common interest and participation in school sport that cement them; they play on the same teams, they practice their craft together in school, and spend weekends and summer holidays playing sport on the same community-based teams. With athletic competence being the key ingredients for group membership and cohesion, entry into the "inner circle of the Jocks" is restricted to a selected few. There are other students who interact peripherally with the clique through their association with the Jocks at the nucleus. For aspiring athletes such an alliance influences their selection onto school teams.

In addition to in-school binding factors, the Jocks' common cultural identity contributes to the cementing process. The shared experiences of early life in Jamaica and the development of cultural competence have fostered a solidarity typical of any minority group in a new environment. Further, living within urban housing complexes where working-class West Indian immigrants are concentrated, the Jocks have drawn sustenance from the community, maintaining whatever cultural resources they have brought along from their country of origin. Factors both inside and outside Lumberville have combined to strengthen the Jocks into a cohesive, formidable social unit within the school environment.

Individually, the Jocks demonstrate varying degrees of opposition to the school's programs and authority structure. But as a group they generate a certain oneness in their dissatisfaction with curricular and extracurricular activities, and more so, the rules and restrictive regulations of the school. Most vocal in such expressions are Weston and Earl, the dominant personalities and leaders in the group. They stand out as the major forces mobilizing antischool and oppositional activities within Lumberville.

With a large percentage of the student population at Lumberville being of a racial minority, the teachers there do not perceive all-black cliques as abnormal. It is the nature of their subcultural group activities that is of most concern to the staff. For example, the attitude and behavior of a notorious group of younger black students labeled "The Bully Boys" and their leader "Nasty" generate much more concern to the staff than the comparatively prosocial Jocks. Furthermore, the contribution of the Jocks to the school's sport program makes it difficult for teachers to classify their group formation as a purely negative influence within the school community at large.

"LANGUAGE IS UNITY, IDENTITY, AND POWER"[1]

People evolve a language in order to describe and
thus control their circumstances, or in order not to
be submerged by a reality that they cannot articulate
(Baldwin 1979).

The language patterns and communicative style among the Jocks and other black students at Lumberville make them a unique and distinct group. Their language form—referred to by names such as patois, "Pidgin English," "Jamaican talk," and dialect—departs from standard English in vocabulary and syntax. Linguists correctly classify this language form as creole with an English-based vocabulary, and with Spanish, French, Portuguese, Dutch and, of course, the African languages contributing to this rich lexicography.[2]

The other difference is syntax; Anglophone-based creole differs from standard English in such ways as grammatical structure, inflection of words, and word order in sentences. Linguists such as Bailey (1966) argue that such differences may have grown out of the need for English planters in the West Indian islands and their African slaves to communicate with each other. Since the use of the African languages was discouraged by the slave owners, a "Pidgin English" evolved in their efforts to communicate with each other. With such African language structures and vocabulary combined with those of Western Europeans and other groups such as the Jews, Lebanese, Chinese and Indian, "Pidgin" developed into a rich West Indian creole that is still spoken today. This language form is popularly known and referred to by its users as patois.

Immigrant West Indian students at Lumberville are very adept in their use of patois and speak it extensively in the classroom, corridors, cafeteria, gymnasium,and on the playground. It dominates school life for two main reasons. First, it is an adequate, functional language for black immigrant children who are more accustomed to speaking this dialect than standard English. Second, it has become a major dynamic in black youth solidarity, excluding authority figures from the communication process. In the classroom, black students show bidialectal skills by responding to the teacher in acceptable English, but communicating with black classmates in patois. Preclass chatter among these students is conducted exclusively in patois, effectively "locking out" teachers and students of another culture and language group. The Jocks are highly articulate in patois and utilize it when communicating with each other in a wide range of situations. One black student explains why: "They do it to belong. They don't want to feel left out. They can speak better [acceptable English] if they want to, but they choose not to."

Horseplay is an activity usually accompanied by subcultural expressions, both by the participants and the "jiving" spectators. The physical interactions

are engaged in by friends, and name-calling such as "nigger" and "black bas-
tard" is routinely exchanged without malice. Both the horseplay and verbal
bantering are symbolic of the solidarity and cultural comradeship that the
Jocks project within the Lumberville school community.

An emerging feature of dialect use among blacks at Lumberville is the
inclusion of "Jamaican profanity" at all levels of discourse. In the West
Indies, incorporation of swear words was limited to the playgrounds, out of
earshot of teachers and other authority figures. At Lumberville, however, its
usage is more widespread. For example, the Jocks greet their friends: "Wa-a-
guan dè, Missa raas claat" [What's going on there, Mr. (profanity)]. Stirred
by excitement in soccer competition, Jocks urge on their team mates, "Come
on, kick the raas claat ball no man!" Miskicks or any such "bad plays" are
met with disapproving hoots and shouts, such as, "Tek yu rass ahfa de fiel, if
yu no know wha yu a do!" [Take your (profanity) off the field if you don't
know what you are doing!]. Appreciation for good plays is also expressed
by, again, shouts of profanity, but in a less menacing tone of voice.

Altercations with opposition players in the heat of competition generate
profane threats in the vernacular as well. In one such incident where an
opposition player made reference to a Jock's mother's "bumbo claat" [anato-
my], a fight erupted and snowballed, with members of each team joining the
mêlée. To the casual observer unaware of the origins and meanings of these
cultural expressions, these verbal exchanges made little or no sense. But
within the culture any negative reference to one's mother will quickly generate a physical altercation.

How do teachers at Lumberville perceive and respond to "Jamaican
talk"? Some jokingly refer to it as "a foreign language called patois." Others
define it as a kind of "American jive," or a language code typical of ethnic
groups. One teacher is confident that immigrant students' poor language is a
reflection of their unschooled background, and that their speech will improve
with proper schooling in Canada. But one teacher explains that the use of
patois in school may sometimes have more to do with disguising communication than low competence in English:

> Teacher: Teachers who have been around for awhile will pick up some of
> the (patois) language. If students say something bad around the
> vice principal he will understand. But I think some teachers just
> write them off [ignore] and wait until these (black) students start
> using "Canadian English" again. And the students know this.
> When they want to get away from what the teachers can under-
> stand, they just break into the patois language again.

Teachers often loathe the use of certain patois phrases that are distinctly
cultural in origin and perceived to be oppositional. In a confrontation between
Weston, one of the Jocks, and a male teacher, Weston snapped at him: "Leave

me alone, no man!" "Don't say 'no man' to me!" was the teacher's retort. While in the Jamaican context the phrase "no man" is just a manner of speaking, the teacher may have been responding, not only to the meaning of the term in this exchange, but to the very subcultural assertion which he found offensive. On another occasion, a teacher's request of a black female student to turn down her "ghetto blaster" was met with a response that utilized vulgar ethnospecific profanity. Although the student's retort was clearly oppositional and rather obscene, the teacher did not respond. In the British context, Driver (1977:356) explains this kind of unresponsiveness:

> The teachers were unable to interpret and respond effectively to the entire range of behaviors and expressions with which the ethnic-minority pupils in front of them were conversant if not highly articulate.

The Jocks' use of double-talk to show opposition to school rules is another feature of language and resistance at Lumberville. The following explanation grew out of a teacher's order to lift, instead of push, a bike along the hallway:

> Weston: She (teacher) said I should lift it up and I go, "You tink mi crazy!"
> She reported to the vice principal that I called her crazy.

In the school, conflict with teachers quickly stimulates the use of patois, albeit offensive. Earl, dissatisfied with the frequency with which his teacher interrupted a videotaped story for explanations, hissed his teeth repeatedly, muttering, "Cho man" [an expression of disgust] several times under his breath. Although the teacher did not respond, a clear message of displeasure with the proceedings was sent "Jamaican style."

Because the West Indian dialect is spoken and understood almost exclusively by students of that culture, their Canadian classmates, as well as teachers, are effectively "locked out." Carby (1982:187), writing about a similar situation in Britain, comments on the teachers' dilemma:

> The ability of black students to use language as a form of resistance can be seen in the teachers' fear of being excluded from communication between pupils; this has always been regarded as an unacceptable loss of authority.

The Jocks see the language issue as a "problem" that extends beyond the school boundaries. The Canadian public's inability to comprehend the messages of resistance communicated through "roots music" [reggae] has given rise to its uncensored circulation. The more seditious types called "rebel music" are usually banned from public sale and consumption in countries such as Jamaica where the "lyrics have meaning." But here in Canada, Weston explains, "most (white) people don't understand it much, only blacks."[3]

The popularity and growth of Rastafarianism, a quasi-religious, quasi-political movement originating in Jamaica, has added a new dimension to

Jamaican creole. In their effort to separate themselves from the "white man's culture" and to reestablish their African heritage and identity, Rastafarians have invented a distinctive form of speech that is both phonologically unique and politically potent. Lowe (1981) explains that the Rastafarians' preference for the word and sound "I" in discourse may be partly because it rhymes with the last vowel of "Rastafari" and also because of their philosophical concern with identity. This has given rise to the popular use of phrases such as "I an' I" meaning "we" or "us"; "I man," and the coinage of other similar sounding words such as "ital" and "irie." At the political level, Rastafarian rhetoric is loaded with messages of resistance and contempt for institutional structures represented by the capitalist employer, the law enforcement agencies, and the school system.

At Lumberville, the Rasta rhetoric is in popular usage among the Jocks and other West Indian subcultural groups. The Jocks often speak of "I an' I" [the speaker and his friend] playing basketball after school, or "feeling irie" (high) after drinking some marijuana tea. At the more oppositional level, the Jocks recall with disgust a confrontation between "I an' I and Babylon system" [the police] who were called to evict them from the school dance. Again, the black youth of Lumberville supplement their resistance to school policies, practices, and programs by playing such reggae music that expresses feelings of injustice, oppression, and subordination.

The Jocks as a group generate social power within the school community because of their competence in dialect use. With almost all the school authority figures and white students effectively locked out of dialect interactions, the Jocks are able to secure for themselves a certain kind of independent power vis-à-vis dominant-group authority figures and students. In Fisher's (1983:126) British research on the use of language in a political context, one West Indian student asserts,

> A fiwe tak dis. Languige is unity, identity an powha [This is our talk. Language is unity, identity, and power].

> ...wite man dem realise di powha in a Rasta an di tak; dat is w'y im wam fi control it in ah school [White man realizes the power in Rasta language; that is why he wants to control it in school].

Initially, Lumberville teachers were as likely as their British counterparts to perceive students' use of West Indian dialect as an indication of their "unschooled immigrant background." But some have since begun viewing this "impenetrable patois" in a political context; a language form that emphasizes opposition to the authority structures of the school, and one that voices dislike for the actions of teachers. Teachers' reaction and response to this "oppositional stance" vary with their individual interpretations of the situation. While some teachers find their own nonresponse an effective way to diffuse the students' power base, others respond with authoritarian measures allocated to them by virtue of their institutional role. So Jocks utilize and elaborate upon language forms from the West Indies in order to assert themselves within an alien school environment, and achieve their own social and political space.

Paradoxically, language in the Lumberville setting functions both to unite and to separate. It pulls together the black segment of the school population, while at the same time alienating those students and teachers who are not of West Indian origin. With almost all of the school administrators, teachers, and white students effectively locked out of dialect interactions, the Jocks are able to secure for themselves a certain kind of power.

DRESS STYLE: FROM "ARMY DIGS" TO "FASHION DREADS"

The Jocks are quite individualistic in their style of dress and appearance. They wear a variety of clothing ranging from the appropriate (according to school guidelines) to the more faddish contemporary fashion in vogue among teenagers. For example, when "army digs" are in, the Jocks wear them; when designer jeans are fashionable, those who can afford them wear them. The more faddish Michael Jackson "sequined glove" worn on one hand and earring worn in one ear were sported by some members of the Jocks when these were fashionable.

The fashion design (sewing) teacher explained that the "jean generation" and "long hair" have been on the decline so these fashions have become an oddity around the school. For some students, the sewing program has been utilized to "make your own." One mother explained:

> For the past five years, that boy (a fashion-conscious Jock) will not wear a pair of cords or a pair of blue jeans. He wears dress pants, tailor-made. He has a coat like the rest of the boys but he'll throw it on only to run across to the store.

The Jocks make an effort to appear well groomed and neatly dressed around the school community. Before leaving each shop class the boys work tediously on their appearance in front of the mirror. Afro combs, a fixture in the boys' pants pockets, become useful in this endeavor. The Jocks enter and leave the building each day with "gym bags" in which they carry their much-needed clothes and equipment for gym and extracurricular sports. A source of complaint in this regard is the "ugly uniforms" issued to them by the school for team sports. They express embarrassment of appearing in inter-school competitions against teams that are more fashionably attired. A popular feature of the Jocks' dress code is the wearing of hats and topcoats beyond the season of usefulness. It is not uncommon to see boys dressed in hats and winter overcoats watching sport events on the playground in temperatures of 70 degrees Fahrenheit and higher.

At the extreme in subcultural appearance are boys, close acquaintances of the Jocks, sporting the "Rasta look," with the cultivated long, braided, or unkempt hair, and beards at various stages of growth. In school, these "locks" or braided hair are kept tucked away under hats, caps, or tams (toques). The wearing of hats in school is prohibited so this style has become another source of conflict with the school authorities. Black youth displaying the "Rasta persona" have been described by British sociologists such as Cashmore and Troyna (1982) and Rex (1982) as "fashion-dreads" or sham versions of the real thing. This is in reference to those youths who wear "dreadlocks" as a matter of fashion, rather than out of religious commitment; and those who adopt the Ethiopian national colors of red, green, and black, signifying black youths' outright rejection of British society.

At Lumberville, these Rasta-looking youths have a strong attachment to the Jocks through sport. They are quite often students who have dropped out of Lumberville and reside in the neighborhood. They are ardent supporters of the school's sports program, and relate to the Jocks as fellow sportsmen. Although the Jocks themselves do not externalize such highly visible subcultural personas, they nonetheless interact peripherally with the "Rasta-types" on and off school property.

BREAKING SCHOOL RULES

The Jocks utilize the classroom, the corridors, the cafeteria, the gymnasium, the playground, and beyond to display a range of behaviors. Activities vary from that of a model student to the most extreme oppositional and counter-school types.

Within the classroom, the Jocks' behaviors are influenced to some extent by the teacher's control approaches. Group interaction is at its highest just before a teacher calls the class to order. Activities include: talking with girls outside the classroom, visiting other classes, and engaging in heated arguments about such topics as sports, girls, reggae music, and teacher "injustices."

The Jocks' behaviors change dramatically from one teacher to another. They may leave one classroom in an orderly fashion and enter the next transformed into counterschool activists. They mill around the teacher instead of going to their seats, they shout at each other, swear, toss projectiles around, crunch up assignment sheets and throw them basketball-style into garbage cans, and bang rulers on top of desks. They wander in and out of their classroom, while friends from other classes pay visits to theirs'. The Jocks show skill in delaying the start of prescribed class work by engaging some teachers in off-topic conversations on sports, exams, school promotion policy, and so on. Another tactic used to slow down work assignments is the demand, in unison, for the teacher's attention and help. While waiting for individual attention, the Jocks wander around the classroom interacting with other students. Substitute teachers, unfamiliar with school routines, are ideal targets for the Jocks to prey on. On occasion, the boys manipulate these teachers into permitting such activities as playing cards instead of doing schoolwork. Clock-watching and "closing books too soon" are techniques used to coerce the teacher into an early termination of lesson presentation.

The school cafeteria at lunchtime is a focal point for counterschool activities. Here, the Jocks engage in queue-cutting instead of joining at the end. Other pranks include tripping up students who go by with lunch trays, name-calling, teasing, trading insults, and chase scenes around the cafeteria, over benches, tables, and out the door. They also make bets as to who can complete accuracy throws, basketball-style, of empty milk cartons into garbage cans. One particular activity appearing to be a major source of conflict between the Jocks and supervising teachers is domino playing, "Jamaican style." In some cultures, domino playing has been characterized as a "kid's game" played by matching dominoes or "pieces." Traditionally, parents and teachers use dominoes as a fun way of teaching arithmetic. Beyond the fundamentals, such mental skills as good memory, concentration, and individual attention are needed to execute successfully. In his book, *Dominoes,* Armanino (1973:3) describes the ingredients of good domino playing:

> (E)ach play presents a new situation and players never think of duplicate hands for guidance. They rely entirely on the ability to analyze each play. The degree of skill that can be applied is limitless and can engage all of your talents. The luck and skill factor are happily so proportional that defeat can always be attributed to luck and victory to skill.

Domino playing "Jamaican style" moves well beyond the "kid's game" and the finer points achieved through skill, guile, and practice. Here, the game takes on a cultural dimension and is often played in a more carnival atmosphere with much fanfare and excitement. Players shout at opponents as well as partners, squirm in their seats, jump up, sit down, wave their "pieces" in the air, then slam them down with gusto on the table. Spectators, awaiting their turn to play, or just enjoying the action, join in this creation of excitement. In tournament situations such a scene would be duplicated several times, with each table of players trying to outdo the other. This style of domino playing, popular in the West Indies and imported into Canada with their immigrants, is very much a popular pastime among West Indians in their communities and schools. Here Weston explains the problems this can create for them in the Lumberville cafeteria at lunchtime:

> You know when you play dominoes you have to slam it down. Mr. Freeman (supervising teacher) came over and said, "Don't slam it down!" Leroy explained to him, "Y'u can't play dominoes without slamming it down." As

Mr. Freeman walked away, we slammed down the dominoes again and
started laughing. Mr. Freeman came back and took me to the principal.

Exclusive knowledge of West Indian-generated rules, and the exaggerat-
ed use of Jamaican dialect make it difficult for other students and teachers to
understand, much less participate in, domino playing. Because of the atmosphere in which the game is played, it is viewed by some teachers as counterschool and thus disruptive to the serenity of the environment. In addition,
domino playing is calculatedly used by the Jocks to display oppositional
behavior and to openly challenge teacher authority. Do such antischool and
oppositional behaviors continue in the gymnasium or on the playing field
that the Jocks call home?

GYM AND PLAYGROUND: THE JOCKS' DOMAIN

The gymnasium is the domain of the Jocks, both as spectators and as participants. During lunchtime, the Jocks and other interested students congregate in
the gym to watch the girls play in intramural sport competitions. As spectators, the Jocks are very vocal, cheering and jeering the female players, shout-
ing obscenities at every play unsuccessfully executed. They sometimes show
disdain for the girls' game by leaving their seats and walking across the gym
floor while a game is in progress. In the spectators' stands they engage in such
counterschool activities as walking about instead of sitting, using foul language, and fondling girls. On one occasion, two Jocks were observed playing
around with switchblade knives, fake stabbing at each other.

As players in the heat of their own competitions, the Jocks' attitude and
approach to the game become more serious. When winning, there is mutual
support and admiration shown by embracing and "palm-slapping" after each
successful play. However, any trace of cohesive teamwork breaks down
under stress. For example, when trailing the opposition players get angry and
quarrel with teammates who "muff" plays. Jocks dispute the referees' decisions and accuse the officials of "unfairness." The opposing players are also
accused of "dirty play" and of trying to injure the Lumberville players. Ani-
mosity between teams leads to ungentlemanly conduct at the end of the
game, with some of the Jocks refusing to shake hands with the opposition.

Subcultural, counterschool activities peak during interschool sport competitions at Lumberville. The logistics of judging events and supervising students make it difficult for the staff to monitor and control behaviors effectively. The following is a description, drawn from field notes, of counterculture activities during track-and-field competitions:

When not engaged in competition the Jocks gather around "ghetto blasters"
on the sideline listening, singing, or dancing to "dub" reggae music. Among

the Jocks' associates are "Rasta looking" boys wearing "dreadlocks" tucked under their hats. Two of the boys rolled "joints" [marijuana cigarettes] openly and proceeded to smoke them with teachers and on-duty police officers nearby. One of them, introduced as "Pusher" asked jokingly if I wanted to buy some "sensemelia" [a species of marijuana].

A few young black women push babies around the playground in strollers. They are acquaintances of the Jocks and interact with them and other black members of the school community. Their familiarity with the social territory at Lumberville gives the impression that they were either present or former students there. Their Jamaican dialect is punctuated by hoots, shouts, laughter, and profanity. Their behaviors are markedly subcultural. The track-and-field events of the day appear secondary to the group's social interaction and subcultural activities in progress on the sidelines. So, for the Jocks and their acquaintances, the gymnasium and the playing field have become sanctuaries for subcultural activities that seriously undermine the behavior norms of the school. Now, let us focus on other areas within the school where such activities run rampant.

CORRIDOR AND HALLWAY BEHAVIORS

At Lumberville, corridors and hallways are enclaves for friends, cliques, or groups. A noticeable feature of student behavior in the hallways is the ethno-racial group segregation into defined areas. The Jocks, for example, appear to claim a particular area as their own territory. Other cliques, both black and white, also stake out meeting points. Territories frequented by black students would earn such names as "Nigger Alley" or "Little Jamaica." It is from these enclaves that students plan and engage in subcultural behaviors.

Crowded corridors and back hallways are areas where horseplay and rowdy behaviors persist. Such behaviors started elsewhere, but usually pick up momentum in the corridors where crowd support is available and reinforcing. One black Student Council member describes the students' inappropriate behaviors inside the school building:

> Gary: Some of them (students) act like real immature children. When you look down the hallway they are running up and down playing tag like they are outside on the playground.

Confrontations that start in classrooms or washrooms usually can be contained there by the staff. However, if they get out of control and move into the corridors, they quickly swell into a mêlée as a growing number of spectators buzz around inciting the combatants on. The following is a description from my field notes of one such confrontation:

About fifty students were milling around and urging on two boys, one black, one white, locked in combat. Teachers stood nervously on the periphery, but were hesitant to intervene. One remarked, "It's too bad one boy [referring to the black fighter] has to give them all [implying black students] a bad name." A glass window shattered. The black boy pointed a piece of broken glass at his opponent, making menacing gestures. The vice principal pulled the white boy away from his assailant and protected him in an office. The black boy pursued, still trying to get at his antagonist. A police cruiser arrived on the scene with two officers. This was closely followed by another cruiser with two more officers. The crowd dispersed. The police appear to be an integral part of the school's maintenance system.

WALL DANCING: CULTURE OR SUBCULTURE?

School dances are also ideal occasions for subcultural behaviors. With the pulsating reggae music, black students demonstrate their competence in reggae dance steps while white students watch, disinclined to participate in reggae dancing that they see as an exclusive black domain. Supervising teachers at these dances frown at the inappropriateness and vulgarity of the dance routines in which the students engage.

> Teacher: There are things that they [black students] do that surprise staff. This "wall dancing" is something that I've not had much dealing with. Grade nine boys lean against the wall, pull girls unto their bodies [into an embrace] and start rubbing up [gyrating] against them. A lot of the girls that I consider nice young ladies were not at all reluctant to participate. When I make them dance in the middle [of the dance floor] some of them ask, "What is the party for?"

Students engaging in such a dance claim it is a cultural activity that can be compared to the more artistic calypso dancing performed in a carnival atmosphere back in the West Indies. If teachers were to censor "wall dancing" participants argue, they would be preventing black students from engaging in a cultural activity in a multicultural society. Faced with such a dilemma, teachers sought assistance from the West Indian community to categorize "wall dancing," either as a cultural or a deviant activity. A common response to this dilemma is that there is nothing cultural about "wall dancing"; students are simply taking advantage of the teachers' ignorance by redefining subcultural activities to suit their own ends.

Students get very oppositional when their "cultural" activities are restricted by the school. Quite often the police are called in to deal with such oppositional behaviors. A teacher related how quickly a black boy will tell a person in authority to "fuckoff." Police called to a school dance to expel "troublemakers" quite often become the target of verbal abuse from students. The teacher concludes that black students' oppositional behavior toward the police is probably generated by their past experiences with these authority figures, but this point of view is expressed by very few teachers within the school community.

BOOZE, HERBS, AND SOUN' SESSIONS

The activities of the Jocks, as a social unit, extend beyond the school site. They congregate at each other's homes where they make plans and engage in a variety of activities. Sitting on street corners listening to reggae music emanating from "ghetto blasters" is also a favorite pastime. Alternatively, they roam around armed with cassette tapes of reggae "dub" music and play them in whatever tape machines are available, in automobiles, in homes, or in portable "ghetto blasters."

[In a group discussion]

PS: What do you guys do for fun when on holidays?

Ike: Sometimes there are parties from ten o'clock at night, and it's still going at 5 o'clock next morning.

PS: What do they do at these parties?

Ike: Smoke ganga [marijuana] and things like that.

PS: How much does it cost?

Ike: It cost alot, man; the guys just bring their own.

Weston: Those guys bring the genuine stuff. But when you go outside and buy, the guys [dealers] mix it with teabags.

Ike: Like Kong; [a pusher] he came to school one day and was selling some ganga. He had it rolled up, you could smell it. They mix it with teabags. I looked at him and laughed.

Weston: There is one mixture that you can't tell the difference. You put serosy (Jamaican herb) and marijuana together because when you drop serosy in the fire it smells like marijuana.

PS: Does it taste the same?

Ike: I don't know (Laughter).

Weston: I drank it [marijuana]. When I was sick my uncle boiled a big pot of it and gave it to me. In about half an hour, I felt better.

Another group activity within the black community is attending basement parties, also called "soun' sessions." Originally, these parties were for friends and acquaintances to have drinks, "smoke a joint," and dance to the latest reggae music from the West Indies. More recently, the hosts of such gatherings have started hiring disc jockeys, charging guests admission fees, and selling refreshments; house parties seem to have become commercial ventures in which friends and strangers mingle together, and the potential for conflict ever-present, as is illustrated below:

[In a group discussion]

> Ike: You ever go to a basement party with gunmen[4] around and all that?

> Weston: Yes. That's why I stop going to parties around here, man. I was upstairs, and I hear, "pow pow" [gunfire]. You want to see guys move [run away], man!

> Ike: There was one guy at Blocker's dance who came up with a little gun.

> Weston: Once we were driving around and we heard one shot, and I said, "I don't like this." Then we saw guys starting to run. We parked the car and came back later on; one of the guys got shot at!

> PS: Did you hear the reason for the shooting?

> Ike: The shooting took place because some guy wouldn't let go of the mike [disc jockey's microphone]. This guy held on to the microphone and said, "ribbit, ribbit." He got hit right in the head with a beer bottle.

> Weston: I don't go to parties around here any more. These parties are not right. I prefer to go to Hamilton.

> Ike: The best time to rip off [steal] a guy's equipment is when you pull a gun and everybody runs. You come back and see the place empty. You see amplifiers and turntables. You can pick up a lot!

Teachers have their own versions of what they consider to be black student deviance outside the school. Within the confines of the staffroom, teachers relate how past students got involved in armed robbery and ended up "doing time" in the penitentiary. Some of these activities are defined by teachers as behavior disorders requiring clinical intervention. Bagley (1979) points out that this is also a popular view with British school teachers who think that black children there show marked prevalence in behavior disorders. Further, Lumberville teachers believe that there is a relationship between the boys' out-of-school and in-school behaviors, the former influencing the latter. Truancy, for example, sometimes occurs among the Jocks who usually stay away from school in groups of twos or threes. While their excuses for absences vary from "sleeping in" to "caring for sick puppy dogs" to "doctor's appointments," teachers are convinced that their absence from school is to pursue clandestine activities. Quite often, when telephone calls are made to the Jocks' homes to verify reasons for absence, the parent or sibling answering the phone is reluctant to reveal the true whereabouts of the absent students. This perceived lack of parent support and cooperation lead teachers to conclude that both parents and their children conspire against the authority structure of the school.

SUMMARY AND CONCLUSION

To summarize, this chapter provides an insider's view of the Jocks and their function within the social system of Lumberville. The most significant feature of this subculture is its employment of ethnospecific behaviors to develop a cultural distinction and identity. These behaviors and attitudes also proved instrumental in separating the Jocks from mainstream norms and values. First, the Jocks' clique formation and membership based on a common immigrant, West Indian heritage provided the basis for separation from the dominant-group students and teachers. This cultural division was further accentuated by the students' practice of setting up and operating within territorial boundaries within the school. Although the boys bought into the commodified youth fashion in vogue within the mainstream, they also embraced the dress style and demeanor of the more radical, antiestablishment "Rasta" subculture. Group identity among the Jocks was further solidified by their use of a restricted language and communication code. The vocabulary and syntax of such a language form was further complicated by the oppositional messages in "double talk" and "Rasta rhetoric." Group formation, dress style, and language ethics became visible markers in group identity and solidarity as well as symbols of separatism from the mainstream culture.

The Jocks further took advantage of their teachers' inability to differentiate between cultural and subcultural activities, thus exploiting weaknesses in these teachers' knowledge base. For example, "wall dancing," inappropriate by school standards, was defended under the guise of "practicing their culture in a multicultural society" while the playing of reggae music above the school's allowable limits was defended on the grounds that such cultural activity has to be performed loudly to be appreciated. Further, the Jocks resisted the arbitrary standards set by the school for the playing of dominoes, a cultural activity, and readily opposed these restrictions in the face of penalty. Thus, the resulting antagonism between the Jocks and the school staff sets the tone for a struggle for power and control within Lumberville. Outside the jurisdiction of the school the Jocks continue to test the limits that society has prescribed for them. Within their neighborhood they engaged in street corner-type activities that border on delinquency. Teachers have projected that such a "culture of delinquency" will bring them in serious conflict with the law, leading to incarceration. Describing the life-style of similar groups of black youth in British schools and communities, Dhondy (1974:47) writes:

Their culture is a day to day affair, an affair of the styles and fashions they collectively generate. They educate themselves within the community and carry their community into the school where one may see them gathered around reggae, developing the social image of their groups.

Emerging from this chapter is an account of the development of a black culture of resistance to the rules and regularities of organized school life at Lumberville. The Jocks employed their "cultural capital," that is, the ethnospecific resources at their disposal, to undermine the school's control strategies and establish their own patterns of behavior.The staff responded somewhat by using the power and authority vested in them to counteract any form of opposition. The next chapter continues to examine the process of interaction between the authority structure of the school and the Jocks' culture of resistance.

CHAPTER 4

Authority, Whites, and Women

Within the social system of the school, the culture that students live affects significantly the quality of the relationship they forge with administrators, teachers, and peers. If students' lived culture is oppositional and resist the rules and regularities of the school, their encounter with the authority structure will be decidedly problematic. In the area of peer relations, research has shown that the quality of dominant-minority group sociability is influenced by the opportunities both groups of students have to interact and the interracial attitudes they bring to these interactions. Such opportunities are sometimes limited by such institutional factors as the schools' differentiation of students for instructional purposes. More importantly, the students' own in-group behaviors and cultural practices become a powerful divisive force. The third area of concern in this chapter is one of gender relations. In multicultural schools, students of different racial and ethnic backgrounds often display attitudes and behaviors toward females that reflect not only their own cultural norms but conflict with mainstream practices. For example, new immigrants such as the Jocks may bring from the West Indies culturally different ways of relating to females from the practices that are customary in the Canadian host culture. The accounts that follow of the Jocks' encounter with authority, whites, and females raise serious questions about the in-school and long-term relationships that are being forged. Does conflict between the school authority and the Jocks' cultural forms lead to distance and alienation between structure and culture? Are the "own group" cleavages so noticeable in multiracial schools a beginning of long-term dominant-minority group dichotomy in society at large? How will the Jocks' practice of gender domination affect their relationship with those females who refuse to accept this as a cultural practice? This chapter explores these themes.

51

AUTHORITY AND POWER

The Jocks perceive teachers [armed with school rules] as antagonists who go out of their way to penalize students. Teachers are labeled judgmental, vindictive, wicked, mean, authoritarian, prejudiced, racists, "crooked" [dishonest], and conspiratorial [scheming]. Heading the list of most despised teacher and chief disciplinarian is the vice principal. With anger and antipathy, Weston describes an encounter with the vice principal that epitomizes some of the labels in popular use.

> Weston: The guy is weird, man! You ask any student in the school, no one likes him.... The guy gave me a detention and I'm going to my locker to check, the guy go, "Five eight-fifteens" [detentions].[1] And I go, "I'm not going to serve no five eight-fifteens for nothing!" And the guy go, "You're suspended!" And the guy told my mother that I swore at him.

Weston's perception is that consequences are handed out arbitrarily by the school authorities, who upgrade detentions to suspensions in rapid succession with no chance of defense by penalized students. This perception was supported by others in a group discussion:

> Boyd: They give you some stupid suspensions. If you miss [do not serve] a detention, they suspend you. And the vice principal sometimes doesn't even want to hear what you have to say. So he just suspend you and call your parents and talking.... You don't get to tell your side of the story, so your parents don't know what really took place.
>
> PS: So Mr. Baxter is the disciplinarian over there, eh?
>
> Boyd: A lot of people told me he doesn't like black people.
>
> PS: What about whites, does he suspend white students the same way?
>
> Boyd: Oh yeah, but not lots though, only one or two. He probably just say, "Go home for the day."

In student-teacher confrontations the Jocks are convinced that the rulings of administrators are always partial to teachers, as this discussion demonstrates:

> Garfield: If there are disputes and it's the student's word against the teacher's, the teacher always gets the upper hand. If the students complain, the V.P. always doubts what they say.
>
> Roy: They [administration] won't take your word; they always take the teacher's story.
>
> Weston: They don't listen to you. They go, "The teacher is always right." That's not fair, man! Sometimes the teacher tells a lie. There is this

guy with the same name as mine who told a teacher to "fuckoff." The V.P. thought it was me and suspended me for five days. When he found out it wasn't me, he suspended the other Weston too, but didn't call me back. I wanted to lik [hit] him in his rass y'u see [physical assault]! When he fool around with me I'm going to pick him up [physical assault]! The guy enjoys getting people suspended!

Ike: The whole school hates him. This guy was going to fill his car's gas tank with sand.

In this venting of feelings the Jocks perceive the teachers' use of power and authority as one way of making student voices nonexistent in conflict situations with the staff. As a retaliation to the use of such arbitrary staff power, students have resorted to swearing at the staff, threatening physical assault, and threatening vandalism against staff property. One immediately gratifying and anonymous way of expressing their sentiment for the vice principal is through the medium of washroom graffiti, "Mr. Baxter is a fag! Mr. Baxter sucks big cocks!"

A Jock expresses the feeling that the vice principal may have been overzealous in restricting the rights of oppositional students and that a conspiracy of silence among teachers allows his arbitrary power and authority to go unchallenged.

Weston: Some of the teachers know he is doing something wrong, but like they say, teacher and teacher stick together. They gonna stick up for him anyway.

The Jocks display caged antipathy toward teachers they perceive as authoritarian, vindictive, and vengeful. Here Weston explains how teachers in the authority hierarchy await the opportunity to exercise the power vested in them by the institution to counteract student behaviors they interpret as nonconformist.

Weston: I just know Mr. Freeman doesn't like me. Once he sent me to the office to talk to the principal about my behavior. The principal said forget about it, and gave me an admit slip to go back to class. Two days passed; Mr. Freeman didn't say anything to me. The third day came, the principal and vice principal were away. This guy, [Mr. Freeman, the teacher next in command] called me down to the office and asked me if I didn't know I was supposed to report back to him when I was sent to the office. I said, "The principal said everything was alright; why should I report back to you?" The guy said, "You have to next time."

Teachers are perceived as overly judgmental. For example, if students are seen waiting in the school office,[2] some teachers hastily conclude that these students are "in trouble," and should have any special school privileges curtailed or withdrawn. If any of these "in trouble" students are school team players, their behavior becomes a factor in their selection to the school team.

Some staff members, however, are perceived positively by the Jocks. For example, the new principal is seen as a sports supporter and the Jocks started lobbying him for improved school conditions.

Group discussion comments verify this:

> Ike: The new principal will go with anything; he is a sports fan. We have a tournament later this month and we think he is coming with us.

> Roy: He will get us into collegiate sports.

> Boyd: Ike is on the Student Council. They ask the new principal to have music in the cafeteria at lunch time. The principal said yeah. If he had asked the vice principal he would have said no, so if there's anything we want, we ask the principal.

While some teachers at Lumberville maintain their social distance from the student body at large, the Jocks have developed a good working relationship with some of the younger male teachers. These are usually coaches of the school's sport teams, and achieving mutual objectives of both coaches and players necessitated positive interaction beyond the classroom. For these few white male teachers, rapport with the Jocks develop to the extent where teacher and students banter on topics as sensitive as race and immigrant-related jokes.[3] For the most part, however, authority relations between the Jocks and most members of the school staff are characterized by alienation, punitiveness, and distance. These social relations in the school are measured by such regularities as the absence of student "say" in staff-student conflicts; the nonnegotiable nature of student consequences meted out by the staff; the insinuation of racial differentiation in the staff approach to student consequences; and the amount of time and effort spent on behavioral control, relative to academic matters.

The Jocks' accounts of their interaction with the staff suggest that the teachers at Lumberville spend a great deal of their time ensuring the student's subordinacy to authority. Bowles and Gintis (1976) assert that it is through these classroom social relationships that working-class students are socialized for their respective future work roles. The Jocks, however, have responded with resistance to any form of subordination, and have shown oppositional behaviors such as threatening physical violence, vandalism against staff property, washroom graffiti, and separatist behaviors by alienating themselves somewhat from the mainstream culture of the school.

BLACK, BROWN, AND WHITE

A salient feature of the peer group social relationships within Lumberville is the limited meaningful voluntary interaction between white and black stu-

dents. Outside the formal in-school groups instituted for instructional purposes, racially distinct small groups are fixtures around the school site:
[From Field Notes]

> A group of black boys is engaged in a "pick-up" game of soccer on the playground. A small group of white boys sat under a tree close by conversing with each other. Inside the school building, black girls gather in groups engaged in discussions utilizing the "patois" dialect form. South Asian (Indian, Pakistani, Vietnamese) groups are less conspicuous because of their smaller representation within the student population. Racial groups operate almost entirely in separate social systems.

One teacher remarks that within Lumberville, where black students, because of their numbers, appear to be the majority group, it is the white students who are isolated and withdrawn. Although there is no overt antagonism between black and white students, there are few interracial friendships. "I don't see much war or fighting because of color. Not that they get along that great; they just don't get in each other's way," observes a teacher.

Sentiments about interrace friendships are also expressed at home.

> Mitch's Mother: Most of Mitch's friends are black. He jeers his bigger brother for having all-white, honky friends all during high school, and even now at college. His twin sister also has mostly white friends.

Mitch's attitude toward his siblings' intergroup relationships, his mother explains, may be a response to their higher-level school placement, and their better integration into the mainstream.

Racial separation at Lumberville is most noticeable in sport. Most school teams are dominated by black students (over ninety percent of the players on the senior basketball, soccer, and volleyball teams are black). The Jocks think white students are uninterested in sports except for hockey, traditionally dominated by whites. Because the school does not have a hockey program, white boys just "hang around and do drugs," one of the Jocks claimed.

What strategies, if any, have the Jocks utilized to dominate this aspect of Lumberville school life? At the level of intramural team formations the Jocks capitalize on their freedom to select and to exclude. Black cliques usually emerge from such a selection process, with white students excluded from the stronger teams or used as "fillers" for weaker teams. In games, team play patterns are structured around cliques. Jocks were observed to involve only their friends, although other team members were in more ideal scoring positions. Quite often, the reluctance of the Jocks to involve white players worked to the detriment of the team as a whole.

In the literature, similar observations have been made in British comprehensive schools where West Indian students have colonized extracurricular sport and regarded this field as their territory. Carrington (1983:58) observes,

"White lads were frequently overlooked unless they were friendly with colored lads in the team." The Jocks' supporters on the sidelines during interschool competitions at Lumberville are almost entirely black students of West Indian origin. Consequently, the Jocks perform for these spectators, entertaining them with ostentatious, showy, individualized, or clique play, rather than utilizing a team approach to the game. While black spectators show their approval by hooting and howling their appreciation, the coach's game plans are ruined by the Jocks' desire to show off. This style is aptly described by their [white] soccer coach as "playing like a Jamaican." Alienated white school peers reject, to some degree, extracurricular sports and are usually not present after school dismissal, even as spectators, to support their black team players. So, while sports bind black athletes and supporters at Lumberville, they provide areas of neutral or even negative value regarding intergroup social relations. This effect was also evident among British multiracial student population (Carrington and Wood 1983).

While extracurricular activities appear to have little effect on positive intergroup relationships, the way the school structures curricular offerings lacks the potential for intergroup contacts. Lumberville's grouping of students according to their level of functioning has contributed, to some degree, to divisiveness in classroom racial composition. For example, the black-white student ratio in the streamed English classes ranged from two blacks and fourteen whites in the top stream, to ten blacks and two whites in the bottom stream. Since students tend to interact and socialize primarily within their class groups (Hallinan and Smith 1985), in-school academic groupings at Lumberville have contributed to the separation of the students along racial-cultural lines.

In other aspects of school activities, the Jocks and other West Indian students are mutually supportive, while at the same time being noncommital to endeavors by whites. This was evident in such activities as fashion modeling and award presentations. Spectators, students, and their parents, seated in distinct racial groups, selectively applauded "their own kind" when these students appeared on stage. In the case of fashion modeling, white students were greeted with the giggles and smirks of black students, while West Indian models were loudly applauded. Relatedly, Louden's (1978) research found that in British schools with a medium to high concentration of blacks, there was a tendency for them to disparage other racial groups. This evident lack of intergroup mutual support has the outcome of distance and even antagonism in black-white social relationships at Lumberville. This low level of interrace-interethnic friendships and the high degree of own-group preferences has been a concern of researchers for many years. Ijaz's (1980) study of differential interethnic attitudes in selected Metropolitan Toronto elementary schools shows that white Canadian children revealed not only own-group preference, but highly negative attitudes toward blacks and other racial minorities.

The Lumberville study points to three in-school factors that foster separatism between the Jocks and their white peers. First, the persistent pattern of grouping for instructional purposes formally separates the majority of black from white students in academic classes at Lumberville. Hargreaves's (1967) study found that student friendships were highly influenced by school tracking, while Troyna (1978) concludes that minority group students who are clustered in low-tracks tended to make in-group friendships. Second, the Jocks' extensive participation in extracurricular sports partially separates them from the majority of white students who tend to define athletic activities as "not theirs." Since the Lumberville boys spent a large segment of their school time involved in sports, the quantity and quality of interaction with white students was limited. Finally, the differentiation in styles and patterns of leisure time pursuits of each group described in chapter three has hindered intergroup interaction. While the Jocks' in-group activities such as playing reggae music, playing dominoes, and shooting basketball strengthen black group identity, they simultaneously alienate others from intergroup relationships. Moreover, top-streamed minority group students wishing to pursue dominant-group, socially prestigious activities, tend to deemphasize subcultural behaviors such as those of the Jocks, and identify more with mainstream cultural values. Such differential commitment to subcultural identity has contributed somewhat to student divisiveness, but this time along black intragroup dimensions.

These patterns support research studies in multiracial schools in Britain (Louden, 1978; Troyna, 1978), the U.S. (Fordham and Ogbu, 1986), and Canada (Adair and Rosenstock, 1976; 1977; McLaren, 1980; Ijaz, 1980) that suggest that students have more favorable attitudes toward their own ethnic or racial groups, and prefer to mix with them in and out of school. Since these "own-group" attitudes develop at an early age and grow stronger in secondary school, there is a real danger that intergroup social relations in low-track Canadian high schools may not improve without planned interventions.

In summary, the cumulative effect of such in-school factors as tracking, uniracial sport participation, and subcultural leisure time pursuits has set the tone for a long-term dominant-minority group dichotomy in Canadian society. The danger perceived is that racial minority groups will turn inward and set up defensive barricades (Hall, 1967).

HOW BOYS DOMINATE FEMALES

What patterns of interaction do the Jocks and their female peers engage in at Lumberville, and in what ways may such interactions affect their gender relationship in Canadian society? Is the Jocks' practice of gender domination a cultural "carry over" from the West Indies, or is it just another subcultural, oppositional response to dominant-group cultural norms and values?

At Lumberville, the Jocks display an attitude of superiority when interacting with their female peers. Girls and their activities are treated as secondary to those of boys'. In sport, girls' events are viewed by the Jocks as
inferior; they complain bitterly that the girls occupy valuable gym space at the
expense of the Jocks' practice time. Why should they share "their gym" with
girls who are not serious about sport? they complained. They demonstrate
open disdain for female sport by walking obstructively across the gym floor
while the girls' intramural competition was in progress. One of their favorite
pastimes was to congregate in the spectator stands during girls' competition
and shout mockingly at the players who did not execute skillfully. For the
Jocks, female sport activities are a provider of boys' entertainment.

Within the structured setting of the classroom, the Jocks have different
ways of exercising control and domination over female students. In the traditional female courses such as home economics, girls are coerced into performing the more arduous tasks of washing dishes and cleaning up work
areas, while the boys themselves settle for duties of less drudgery. In territory control there is the tendency for the Jocks to dictate the seating patterns of
female students by establishing seating boundaries that girls will not violate.
The Jocks also exercise control over the acceptability of certain behaviors in
the classroom. For example, girls applying makeup were severely criticized
for turning the classroom into beauty salons.

In sports, the Jocks are reluctant to engage in any activity that does not
carry a macho image; they denounce badminton as a "sissy game" and are
skeptical about playing it. Their sexist bias was again demonstrated by their
reluctance to take the sewing course, suggesting that they would be perceived
by others as effeminate or "gay." After the mandatory junior year enrollment
in sewing, none of the Jocks elected to continue this program as an option.

The Jocks and other black boys often engaged in boisterous and sometimes physical encounters with girls of similar West Indian background. In
these encounters girls are grabbed, shoved against the wall, and sometimes
fondled. Girls responded in different ways to their aggressors. Some shout
objections, but appear to make no genuine effort to disentangle themselves
from the boys' grasps. The boys, therefore, rationalize the girls' responses as
reciprocal. While to the onlooker interactions may appear inappropriate and
loaded with sexual meaning, the aggressors claim that these behaviors are
culturally appropriate, and are their way of practicing "comraderie." Within
the sociocultural framework of Lumberville, these black, working-class girls
are clearly dominated, and as Willis (1977:46) describes it, they appear to
"collude in their own domination."

There are other female students who, although they find these inappropriate encounters with boys distasteful and a violation of their bodies, feel power-
less to prevent it. They also conform to group pressure. One such female student articulates her powerlessness by stating, "The boys know some girls are

too embarrassed to report to the teachers what the boys do, so boys just continue the harassment and get away with murder." A third category of female students, however, refuse to collude in this domination and respond aggressively to the boys' advances. They swear at, hit, and throw objects to ward off offenders. In addition, some have established a self-defense network by banding together to protect themselves from the boys' physical harassment. Female students who do not submit themselves to domination reap the full wrath of the Jocks, as this information from an individual interview shows:

> Roy: All the girls there [at Eastway School] I hate. If I go to Eastway, for the first couple of days I'm going to smack out a couple of girls, man. They are too damn mouthy! These girls are too wild, they need a man to cool them down. When they all get together they begin talking and making noise, but when they are not in a group, they are nice and quiet.

Roy's concern about the group behavior of girls was evident on days of Lumberville's outdoor activities. On such social occasions, when subcultural behaviors are at the maximum, groups of black girls would shout at, and trade obscenities and vulgarities with any group of boys. It may be these realities that inspired Weston to write the following (in his Poetry Book):

> A bee may kiss his honey,
> A millionaire can kiss his money,
> A trout may kiss a bass,
> And you, my girl, can kiss my ass.

The Jocks' culture of male dominance operates beyond the school and in their homes where, quite often, some assume the adult role of male authority in the absence of a father figure. They treat their mothers, some of whom are sole parents, with the same attitude of male superiority as they show female peers at school. This is evident from the following explanations:

> Roy's mother: He (Roy) feels that he is a man and doesn't need Mommy to stand behind him.... So I understand that a boy can't come to Mom and talk to Mom like Dad, but I told Roy a few years back, "If you need a man to talk to, Roy, I'll go out and find you a man to talk to."

In addition to marginalizing the female role in the mother-son relationship, the Jocks sometimes assume the authority to screen and communicate to their mothers only that school information they wish to convey. They have also taken the responsibility of decision making, presiding independently over their own schooling and thus their own futures.

[In an interview with Roy]:

> PS: What does your Mom think about your decision to transfer to another school?

Roy: I just told her I'm going to York Park, and that's that. She asked me
      why and I told her that that school is more interesting.

PS: What about Mitch, is that the school he will be attending?

Roy: They won't let him in. He didn't tell his Mom he didn't earn even
      one credit [toward a secondary school diploma].

PS: So his mother doesn't even know what's going on?

Roy: No, she doesn't.

The Jocks' attitude of superiority over females in the Canadian context
may have its roots in the social formation of the West Indies. Foner's (1979)
and Christiansen, Thornley-Brown, and Robinson's (1980) studies document
the experiences of sexual domination by males there, and paint pictures of
the physically demanding and financially unrewarding lives of women in the
West Indies. Conversely, men's lives are perceived to be much more pleas-
ant and less arduous. The assumptions that West Indian and Black American
kinship systems are matriarchal may be based on women's important role in
the family. Anthropoligists prefer the term "matrifocal" since martriarchy by
definition means "publicly recognized power and authority surpassing that of
men" (Rosaldo and Lamphere 1974:3). Evidence of such a "matriarchal"
society in the West Indies and elsewhere is hard to find, Tanner (1974) concludes. A close examination of interaction patterns between black mothers
and their adolescent sons and daughters gives some insight into the structure
of consciousness carried from the West Indies. Accounts of family life in
Canada and the sexual division of labor within the home show that boys,
more so than girls, enjoy a greater freedom from such domestic commitments as childcare, cleaning, and cooking. In addition, boys are given more
independence in deciding how they spend their free time. More importantly,
the boys in this study are given greater freedom than their female siblings to
make educational decisions. For example, one mother explains that she
quickly intervened in her daughter's unproductive schooling by withdrawing
her from Lumberville and sending her to "learn a trade." For her son, Ike,
however, the decision to stay or leave Lumberville was left to him.

The Jocks' culture of male dominance in the Canadian context appears
to be supported inadvertently by their mothers' own formation of consciousness taken from the West Indian society. Fuller's (1982:94) study of the double subordination (female and black) in British society found female siblings
resentful of their brothers' assumed superiority:

> With amused disbelief most girls said boys considered themselves superior
> to girls: "...most West Indian boys definitely aren't going to let a woman
> dominate them and tell them what to do, they firmly believe they're the
> boss and she has to do everything.... They just have this thing that they are
> the superior ones and women inferior."

The Jocks' effort to project male dominance in the Canadian society may be more than a "cultural hangover" from the West Indies. In a Canadian social formation characterized by white dominance, black boys' furtherance of patriarchal relations of gender domination may be one way of reasserting the power taken away through racial subordination. The reassertion of power, however, has taken on decidedly subcultural and oppositional dimensions that extend well beyond the relations of patriarchy. Girls are sexually exploited and their rights and freedom severely restricted by behaviors the Jocks define as "practicing comraderie." Such action may be no more than subcultural activities masquerading as culture. The Jocks' subordination of females may also be seen as acts of opposition to dominant-group cultural norms and values. Minorities who experience subservience within an established social order will refuse to conform to such dominant-group codes of behavior.

SUMMARY AND CONCLUSION

To summarize, this chapter contributes to the thesis that the forces of structure and culture within Lumberville contribute to a massive social and cultural differentiation between authority figures, dominant-group students, and females on the one hand, and the Jocks on the other. Conflict and tension characterize the relationship between the school's authority structure and the Jock's lived culture, and there was the tendency for institutional structures to become more rigid and restrictive and cultures to be strident in their opposition and resistance. The punitiveness, alienation, and distance that result from such an interaction severely limit the Jocks' educational and, in the long run, life opportunities. Furthermore, the in-school relationship between the authority structure and the Jocks will set the tone for the way the Jocks will function in the world of work. Bowles and Gintis's (1976) treatise on schooling for the workplace has drawn attention to the striking similarity in the structures of authority in school and in the workplace. Willis's study has shown that subcultures that circumvent the maintenance system of the school have responded similarly to the authority structure on the shop floor. The projections are that the Jocks' culture and life-style will be at variance with the established social order at their place of employment.

In the area of intergroup interaction, the Jocks show very little meaningful social relationship with their white peers and operate almost entirely within a separate cultural system. There appears to be little voluntary social relationship between the white and the West Indian students in the larger school population. At the subcultural level, the Jocks exclusionary extracurricular activities and leisure time pursuits do little to foster intergroup relationships. The structure of groups for academic instruction and the students' pattern of "own group" friendship have laid the foundation for a long-term dominant-minority group dichotomy in the Canadian society at large. The blurring of intergroup boundaries and the unrestricted interaction between students of different racial and ethnic subgroups are not likely to come about without planned intervention at the school and community levels.

The final area of focus in this chapter is what McRobbie (1980:40) terms the "collective disregard for women and the sexual exploitation of girls" by a male, working-class subculture. Whether the Jocks' domination of females was motivated by the West Indian cultural legacy of patriarchy or the urge to oppose dominant-group cultural norms and values, the in-school and long-term effects on gender relations will be antagonistic. This study shows that while mothers who are socialized in the West Indian patriarchal culture may accommodate their sons' dominating behavior, females socialized in the dominant Canadian culture were less accommodating. Not only have they socially differentiated themselves from the Jocks, they have also developed strategies to combat what they perceive as rebelliously inappropriate behaviors that subordinate them and violate their rights.

This examination of the Jocks' relationship with authority figures, white students, and females within the arena of the school reveals a kind of social and cultural differentiation with the potential for long-term separation from the mainstream culture. The next chapter explores a more proschool dimension of the Jocks' separatist activities and the factors in and outside Lumberville that contribute to this process.

CHAPTER 5

Sport as Work

> Basketball needs black kids and black kids need basketball.... More black kids
> are staying in high school. Some of these will use basketball to take them
> beyond high school. Some of them will be looking at U.S. scholarships.
> (The C.B.C. "The Inside Track")

This chapter moves beyond the Jocks' oppositional frame of reference and
examines their more prosocial athletic life at Lumberville. The literature on
student life in multiracial schools has indicated the tendency for black students, more so than whites, to embrace physical education and extracurricular sports. Such a black-white dichotomy in sport participation may have had
its beginnings in the "white mind, black body" ideology that pervaded educational thought in the United States at the turn of this century. Tyack (1974)
argues that intelligence testing provided the technology for the stereotyping
of whites as mentally superior to blacks and blacks as "hand minded" and
"motor minded." Curriculum planners, anxious to reduce and cure truancy
among "motor-minded" blacks in inner city schools, instituted a strong program of physical education and athletics in their vocational and technical
schools. This association of blacks with physical rather than mental agility
gained support from the eugenics movement and still influences the attitudes
and behaviors of teachers and students alike today (Kane, 1971; Selden,
1978).

Here, we examine the extent of the Jocks' involvement in school athletics
and explore what motivating factors are behind such a preoccupation. What is
the role of the school in this sponsorship and socialization process? Is sport used
as a control mechanism, curbing, containing, and neutralizing black resistance
to the authority structure of schools as Lawson (1979) suggests? How does such
intense involvement affect their participation in other curricular endeavors and
their acquisition of academic credentials? The career aspirations of the Jocks
and their prospects for postschool occupational placement in the Canadian labor
market will be examined against the backdrop of the quality of their school cur-

riculum, the choice of vocational options available to them, and their introduction to the work force through part-time and summer employment.

THE SPORT SUBCULTURE

The Jocks' school life was completely immersed in the sport subculture. As
the following field notes show, their involvement was intensely routinized:

> Preclass workout each morning was followed at lunchtime by intramural
> athletic competitions in which the Jocks either played or officiated. Imme-
> diately following classes, the Jocks took part in either tryouts for school
> teams, team practices, or competitions. For tournaments and other inter-
> school league programs, the Jocks and other school team members were
> excused from academic instruction to represent their school.

This preoccupation continues throughout the school year starting with
"vocational school" soccer in the fall and rotating to basketball, volleyball,
badminton, track-and-field athletics, and "collegiate" soccer toward the end
of the school year. When not physically participating, the Jocks are mentally
tuned into sports, grasping every opportunity to discuss topical issues.

Beyond the boundaries of the school, the Jocks continue their intense
involvement. Evenings and weekends are spent in the community gymnasium and on the playing field, practicing and perfecting their skills in basketball, volleyball, soccer, and baseball. During the summer holidays, the Jocks
join community-sponsored sport teams and participate in intercity leagues
and tournaments. Parents attest to the Jocks' intense involvement in sports
outside of school:

> Roy's Mother: Roy is a boy who is always into sports. In the summertime
> he is always over there in the field playing this and that. He
> is gone for the whole day long.... But it's good for him;
> he's happy.

Another pastime of the Jocks is tuning in to televised professional
sports. Here, they become animated as they admire and cheer on their
favorite stars. It is commonplace to hear the Jocks recall with accuracy the
details of games they watched on television. The centrality of sports in the
lives of the Jocks at home, in the community, and at school was borne out by
Roy's refusal to accept the much sought-after promotion to a higher-track
school because curricular sports were not timetabled:

> Roy: I was going to attend Eastway [high school] and I forgot to choose
> sports [Physical Education] as an option. When I went back to
> change my schedule I couldn't get sports anymore, so I didn't accept
> the promotion to Eastway. If I don't have gym I'm spaced out, I'm
> bored to death.

For other Jocks, involvement in sports was not simply to overcome boredom or to provide entertainment; they accommodate aspirations of becoming career athletes, as Boyd divulges:

[In an Individual Discussion]

> PS: What kind of job are you preparing to do later in life?
>
> Boyd: I play hockey, right? I play good hockey...
>
> PS: Do you think you could get a job as a pro hockey player?
>
> Boyd: Yeah, 'cause I am a M.P.W.H.A. [Metro Pee Wee Hockey Assn.] player, so I'm on camera and everything. I'm good enough to play for Father Henry [school] but they are Catholics and I'm not.[1]

To become professional sportsmen, the Jocks argue, means acquiring athletic scholarships to colleges in the United States. The way to acquire such scholarships is to attract scouts who travel around the Metro Toronto high schools seeking out talented players. Attending school at Lumberville makes exposure to scouts problematic; these scouts do not visit vocational schools. The head of the Physical Education Department at Lumberville explains:

> Yes, the boys do aspire to be professional athletes. But the fact that they are in a vocational school that does not prepare students for college is an indication of their unrealistic expectation...

Faced with this reality, the boys have become primarily obsessed with leaving Lumberville for other schools that will give them the opportunity to realize their objectives in sports.

> Ike: I am expecting to leave this year to go to York Park or Yorkville. Roy [another Jock] wants to go, too.
>
> PS: Why Yorkville?
>
> Ike: They have sports at that school, and my friend goes to York Park.

Parents and teachers have responded with pessimism to the Jocks' aspirations to become career athletes:

> Mitch's Mother: At one time Mitch really thought he could win a sport scholarship, but that is no longer a realistic expectation.
>
> Physical Education Teacher: The trek of boys to schools such as York Park is in chase of an elusive dream. Many of them cannot make it there and have returned [to Lumberville] to hang around.

Such pessimism has been supported by research findings. In the United States, Harry Edwards (1988:138) has presented precise and revealing data:

> Only five percent of high school athletes go on to compete in their sports at the collegiate level...which is to say that over ninety-five percent of all ath-

letes must face the realities of life after sports at the conclusion of their last
high school athletic competition.

Focusing on the black athlete, Edwards's data show that for those who
went to college on athletic scholarships, sixty-five to seventy-five percent
never graduate from the school they represent in sports. And the most
startling career statistics for black high school students who aspire to be
career athletes is that only 1.6 percent (less than two out of a hundred) of
those blacks that participated in collegiate football, basketball, or baseball
ever sign a professional contract. Edwards's concluding point is that within
three-and-a-half years over sixty percent of those who sign contracts are out
of professional sport (p.140).

The Jocks view the pursuit of sports as a vocational option in the same
way they perceive a job in industry. If their aspirations are grounded in reality
rather than fantasy, these boys have not accumulated any background information regarding requirement for entry, necessary training, and employment
possibilities after training. Furthermore, career counselling services, whose
function is to provide students with useful information necessary for them to
make informed career choices, have no data on "career athletics" or related
fields, thus making informed choices even more difficult for the Jocks. Even
for higher-track, college-bound athletes, chances of a career in professional
sport are remote.

> Physical Education Teacher: The percentage of kids that ever make it to a
> professional sport is less than a half of one
> percent coming out of high school; except in
> hockey with which a vast percentage of blacks
> have little to do.

This view is supported by researchers on black youth and sport in
Britain. Cashmore (1982:217) emphasizes:

> The chances of making sport into a career are extremely limited: At the
> time of writing little more than fifty blacks can claim to earn a full time liv-
> ing from sport. True, they may be conspicuous and indeed, lionized but...
> there are thousands upon thousands of unsuccessful black would-be sports-
> men, with careers in threads, having placed too much hope on the precari-
> ous sporting world.

The Jocks' desire to transfer to other Metro high schools is also a result
of their dissatisfaction with Lumberville's sports program. Their discontent
ranges from their limited participation in interschool competitions, to the
value of their rewards for representing their school, to their coaches' lack of
dedication to sports.

[Group Discussion]

> Weston: We want more games; maybe one game this week and one next
> week.

Ike: Or just practice a few days and play about two games... like regular high schools.

Roy: Yeah, basketball is our biggest sport, but we play only one tournament. All that time we have to sweat [work hard]!

Ike: Just for a one-day tournament, and you don't get nothing.

Weston: We don't get any trophy at this school [Lumberville].

Roy: Only a ribbon and a banquet.

Weston: We don't even get a trophy.

For their dedication to sports and their contribution to the school's athletic program, the Jocks have won individual awards each year. For two consecutive years, members of the group were awarded such sport honors as, "Athlete of the Year," a "Special Award Plaque," an "Honor Athletic Letter," and a "Second Athletic Letter." These awards are presented at the annual sport banquet; but as the boys complained, their prizes are merely symbolic gestures and are of no practical value. For example, Lumberville's athletic awards do not win them places in higher-track (academic) schools, or guarantee them a spot on higher-track school teams. The Jocks have argued vehemently for soccer to be a part of their spring athletics program. This scheduling would enable them to compete with collegiate teams, giving them the exposure they seek. This change, however, is incompatible with other extracurricular sport programs within the school.

[In a Group Discussion]

Roy: There are a lot of schools around here we could play.

Weston: When we ask them [staff] to play, man like "No, no, no." We never got the chance to [play against other schools]!

Ike: Like in the spring when we are going to play soccer—Mr. Brown (Head of Physical Education) thinks it will interfere with the track-and-field program.[2]

The focus of the group discussion on scheduling problems shifts to school personnel. The Jocks accuse the track-and-field coach of protecting his domain at the expense of their future in soccer.

In addition to the Jocks' perception of the coaches' selfishness, they also evaluate the coaches as lacking in the motivation to commit Lumberville teams to tournaments that involve travel.

Ike: Like, the gym teachers are lazy. They don't want to take us anywhere.... I heard Yorkville [another vocational high school team] was in Ottawa last Friday or Saturday, and they are going to Quebec this year.

The Jocks perceive laziness on the part of teachers for running intramural competition at lunchtime instead of after classes. They claim unsupervised practices for school team players are limited because students are not permitted to use the gym without staff supervision. Some coaches were criticized by the Jocks for their lack of interest in interschool competition. Such criticisms vary from charges of selfishness, laziness, and apathy to incompetence. The Jocks blame the loss of key games in basketball tournaments on tactical errors in offensive and defensive formations made by the coach.

AGENTS OF SPORT SOCIALIZATION

What is the role of the school in the black students' sports aspirations and participation? The Lumberville structures and the extracurricular sport program encourage students' participation through special incentives and awards. Although such structures encourage participation, there is no evidence that teachers set unrealistic expectations for the Jocks and other black students in their school. To the contrary, some teachers at Lumberville question the merits of interschool athletic competition:

Physical Education Teacher: Even now at Lumberville, there is a whole debate going on as to whether or not these kids should be competing in a [higher-track] league, and I have my own personal feelings about that.

PS: What are they?

Physical Education Teacher: I don't see them as being able to compete in higher-track [collegiate] sports. I don't personally believe that they have the ability, the mental capacity to compete at that level. And then you can also get into their emotional stability to withstand fairly intense competition at that level.

Teachers' low expectation of the mental ability and emotional stability of students in this school limit students' opportunity to participate in sports beyond high school. Even at higher-track schools coaches are not very optimistic about students realizing their dreams of sports as a money earner.

Why then does Lumberville instigate and sustain the black students' interest in sports? The Jocks' participation in this structured extracurricular activity is inextricably linked with their academic work effort and their commitment to the school's codes of behavior. Teachers often bring to the forefront of athletes' consciousness the message that incomplete or unsatisfactory school work will jeopardize their position on school teams. The challenge facing the Jocks here is trying to ascertain and maintain the arbitrarily set standards of performance demanded by teachers. For example, the physical education teachers and coaches with their vested interest in the Jocks' athletic abilities would be less rigorous than their fellow teachers in scrutinizing the Jocks' academic performance.

However, it is commitment to the school's codes of behavior that athletic privileges are closely linked. Unpunctuality and absenteeism carry the penalty of suspension from school teams; reinstatement depends not only on improvement in attendance and punctuality, but also on the discretion of the coaches and school administrators. Any kind of oppositional behavior that threatens the authority structure of the school would result in suspension or exclusion from school teams. Again, enforcement of the written and unwritten rules would be carried out arbitrarily by teachers, thus putting tremendous pressure on the Jocks to determine the margin between acceptable and unacceptable behavior. Thinly veiled threats of removal from school teams carry a neutralizing effect on any oppositional activities of the Jocks.

At the other end of the social control continuum is the reward system. In addition to the privilege of representing the school in sports, the school encourages good work effort and behavior by promises of sponsorship to higher-track schools with a wider selection of athletic activities. The most visible rewards, however, are the annual awards to athletes for good sportsmanship and good citizenship. From the examination of the relationship between sports, the enforcement of the school codes of behavior, and academic work habits, there is a strong indication that Lumberville exploits the Jocks in their most vulnerable area: the love of school sports. Such a control strategy is a crucial factor in the balance of power between black resistance to schooling at Lumberville and the authority structure of the school. This issue will be further explored in chapter seven.

Lumberville's use of sports as a neutralizer of black resistance may be related to its teachers' perception of black students as being more naturally talented physically than intellectually. The disproportionate number of black students meeting the school's I.Q. criteria for low-track placement contributes to this perception. This stereotyping was further demonstrated by the coaches' reluctance to expose black athletes to sports such as football, and the "complicated play patterns" of basketball that they claim require mental agility. On the other hand, black students' overrepresentation in Lumberville's sport programs confirm teachers' belief that they have natural physical ability. Over ninety percent of the school's senior basketball, soccer, and track-and-field teams are black. They dominate other areas of extracurricular sport. This domination is not unique to Lumberville; in other mixed-race schools in urban Canada, preliminary research shows that black students are overrepresented in team sport.[3] In Britain, one of Cashmore's (1982:106) black respondents summarized the effects of teacher expectations on student achievement:

> Teachers definitely think of you as a good athlete if you are black. They seem to have this idea about natural talent and any [black] kid who shows the slightest promise is put into sport and made to concentrate on that.

Teacher expectations, therefore, influence educational practice in multiracial schools. At Lumberville, teachers have invested much time and effort, relative to that spent on academics, developing black students' athletic potential. These endeavors contribute to the erection of barriers to academic opportunity within the school for this racial group.

Beyond the socializing environment of the school and its teachers as agents, the media has become an influential force in projecting and publicizing black professional athletes as role models. Black children are bombarded by the images of black superstars in such sports as basketball, football, baseball, soccer, boxing, cricket, and track-and-field athletics. These images have significant impact on the psyche of black children who internalize them as proof of success for "their kind." For instance, modeling within the basketball milieu of the black community in urban Canada is captured cogently by a social commentator:

> [M]any of these [black] kids dream of playing in the NBA (National Basketball Association). They call their idols by their first names: Michael [Jordan], Magic [Johnson], Isiah [Thomas], Dominique [Wilkins]. For many of these kids, this gym is a getaway... (CBC's "Sunday Morning")

When not directly engaged in athletics, the Jocks at Lumberville use every available opportunity to discuss the unique qualities and the latest feats of their favorite stars. They also spend much time watching their idols on television or reading about them in *Sports Illustrated* and in the newspapers. A teacher at Lumberville is convinced that there is some relationship between the media's glamorization of black athletes and black students' aspirations to be career sportsmen:

> Teacher/Coach: Part of the reason for getting this business of professional sports [among students] is the predominant number of blacks in the media playing professional football, baseball and basketball.... The examples are there for these kids when they watch professional sports on T.V. Players in the high exposure positions are usually black.

The notion of black athletes highlighted in the media as models is supported by British teachers who recognize that black sportsmen often constitute "significant others" for black youth. Carrington (1983:52–53) quotes one such teacher, "West Indian pupils identify with black sportsmen. Maybe it's the influence of television. They have suddenly realized they're good at something." Cashmore (1982:215) points out that "black youth use successful figures as blueprints for their own development. They engage in role modeling, organizing their personal aspirations and commitments around visible models."

Conspicuously absent from the list of significant others who encourage and nurture black youths' obsessive pursuit of athletic goals are their parents. For the Jocks at Lumberville, this was not surprising since parents were not sufficiently involved in the schooling process to fully understand the extent of their sons' preoccupation and the possible long-term consequences of such an involvement with school sport. Their awareness is limited to triumphs when special athletic awards are won by their sons. In the past, unfortunately, these parents have not assessed the academic costs at which awards are won; little do they know of the countless hours, during and after school, that students invest in athletics. More recently, however, such concerns expressed by blacks in multiracial school communities such as those in Britain and the U.S. have filtered through to the black community leaders in Canada. Through such mediums as their ethnic associations and newspapers, parents are slowly developing an awareness of how their children's preoccupation with school sports is limiting their time spent in the classroom. Such realization by the parents of the Lumberville Jocks has yet to be translated into action militating against the socialization process.

What is the role of students themselves in the socialization process? The data suggest that by their attitudes and behaviors both white and black students at Lumberville nurtured the myth of black superiority in athletics. The following dialogue recorded at the beginning of the soccer season is evidence of this belief:

> PS: Are there a lot of white guys trying out for the school [soccer] team?
>
> Harry [white student]: About ten to twelve out of twenty-five guys, but the majority of those who make the team are black.
>
> PS: Why is this so?
>
> Harry: Maybe the white guys are not as good as the black guys.

The myth of black superiority in sport is shared by Leroy, a member of the Jocks, "They [white students] don't want to come out [to practice]. Some of them are not good."

From these attitudes and beliefs, white "would-be" athletes withdraw from school sports and concede to the black athletes they perceive as superior. Black students, in the meantime, grasp the opportunity to use sports to validate their black identity. This is not a difficult task for them to accomplish. They are motivated by images of successful black athletes in the media and prospects of employment opportunities. In addition, they are helped along by teachers and coaches who create the opportunity structure to "develop their talents."

McPherson's (1970) three elements of the socialization process prove useful in summarizing this section (see figure 2). First, the personal attributes of the Jocks, their attitudes and internalized social values, make them ideal candidates for immersion into sports. The second element, socializing agents, is most significant for this study. Teachers and coaches at Lumberville disagree among themselves and with the Jocks on the quantity, quality, and purpose of a program that provides the opportunity structure for the Jocks to overindulge in athletic activities. Despite such disagreements, socializing agents are nonetheless an influential factor in the Jocks' socialization into sport roles.

FIGURE 2
Jocks' Socialization Into Sports

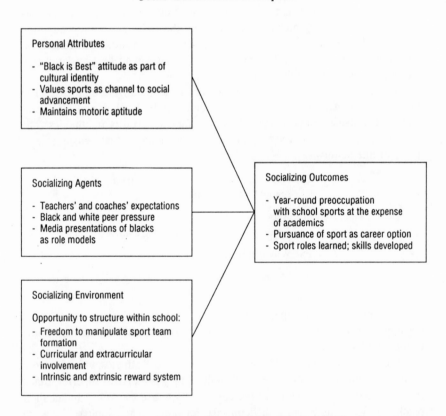

Adapted from B. D. McPherson (1970): *The Three Elements of the Socialization Process*

In the case of the Jocks at Lumberville, the outcome of such a socialization process is twofold. The short-term outcome is a complete preoccupation with the sport subculture and a diversion away from the pursuit of academic credentials. The long-term consequence of such disengagement from the academic curriculum may well be one of future socioeconomic marginality. Evidence of such a consequence is captured in a Lumberville teacher's description of one student's transition from "star athlete" to school dropout into the world of marginalized labor:

> This student lived, ate, slept basketball; he always had a basketball in his hand. He ended up making the all-star team; but as he got older his focus changed quickly from sports to earning money. He dropped out of school to earn money.

WORK: LIFE AFTER SPORTS

The employment aspirations of the Jocks are laden with contradictions. What proves most problematic is the incompatibility of their career aspirations with their low-track placement in school. The ambiguity that arises from Boyd's ambitions to become a "professional hockey player or an office cleaner" in the same breath is also evident in other students' responses to queries about their future goals:

> PS: Is there any particular job you have in mind when you leave school?

> Leroy: Well, first I want to go into weightlifting or something. I wouldn't mind going to college and studying attorney.

Byron, a grade twelve student nearing graduation, prefers not to go the route of promotion to Eastway and into the job market. Instead, his ambition is to attend a career-oriented community college. Byron, however, had not explored the entry requirements for the program in which he would like to enroll, although nearing high school graduation.

Invariably, the shop programs in which the Jocks are enrolled at Lumberville will not prepare them for the career goals they are aspiring to achieve, as is evidenced from the following interview about jobs:

> PS: What kinds of jobs are you thinking of doing when you graduate from school?

> Mitch: Cabinetmaking; but now I'm considering autobody or automechanics.

> PS: If you can't get a job in cabinetmaking, what other can you do?

> Mitch: Autobody or automechanics.

It must be specially emphasized that Mitch's school history indicates that he had not taken courses in either of these areas, yet he has listed them as career alternatives to cabinetmaking, a course in which he was enrolled. Another Jock expressed the career ambition to be an automechanic, yet has taken no shop courses in that field and does not intend to enroll in the near future.

A number of Jocks, even though nearing graduation, are either uncertain about the careers they wish to pursue or have not given it any thought. When some parents get an indication that their sons are not making any career decision by their final year of high school, they interrogate:

> Mother: I ask Roy a hundred thousand times, "What do you want to be? You've got to try for a trade or something. There is John Brown College that you can go to for all kinds of things." But he still hasn't come up to me and said, "I want to do this."

Harvey's (1980) study of students' employment and school related attitudes reveals that a little over a quarter (27 percent) of Lumberville students intended to enter the occupational fields of processing, machining, fabricating or related industrial occupations. But, the same proportion (27 percent) "…were not sure of the type of work they intend to seek when their education is completed" (p.36).

School attendance by the Jocks and other students at Lumberville is often interrupted by job hunting or actual part-time employment. It is customary for students to attend classes in the mornings and go to work in the afternoons in such places as restaurants, factories, and retirement homes. Some students attended school on a full-day timetable then went directly to jobs where they worked until about midnight. Others worked beyond the holidays into school time, as revealed in this interview:

> PS: Did you work during the summer holidays?

> Roy: I worked at Direct Transport loading and unloading trucks. I am still working there now.

> PS: When are you starting back at school?

> Roy: Well, the 14th of September. That's when it [work] stops. Then it will probably take a while for me to get back [to school].

Here, the work completion date dictates when this student returns to school. The Jocks are constantly juggling school and work to arrive at a compatible arrangement. Some have had to suspend part-time work to continue schooling—as Earl points out, "I had to give up my last job because they [employer] wanted me to work the morning shift." Despite this setback, Earl has continued to search for a part-time job that will not conflict with his schooling and thus ruin his chances of receiving an education: "I'm looking for work; I'm always trying to get a job at the Shoreline [hotel]. I'll do any kind of job right now, even office cleaning."

[And, from another individual interview]

> PS: Where are you looking for a job?

> Byron: Downtown. My mother said I should go to gas stations, fill out some applications and see what happens.

> PS: I heard that you have a part-time job right now. When do you go, and what do you do?

> Byron: I go Tuesdays, Wednesdays, Thursdays, and sometimes Saturdays. You know those flyers and stuff? We pack them together, weigh them, and put them in trucks.

> PS: How long have you been working there?

> Byron: About three months now, working five hours per day earning about $3.50 an hour.

This kind of work schedule pressured Byron to rush away after school, missing some of the extracurricular sport programs in which his schoolmates participated.

Parents encourage their children to find part-time work and summer employment, and are pleased when their efforts are rewarded.

> Roy's Mother: Roy had a couple of summer jobs, and he is a good little worker from what I've heard. He worked up at Wonderland washing dishes and cooking.... Then he worked down at the race track doing a bit of everything, and again washing dishes. He is the type of kid that will work without supervision when he is shown how to do something.

The motivation of the Lumberville Jocks to seek out low-skilled, low-paying employment contrasts with the antipathetic attitude of young, second-generation blacks in Britain toward such work. Dhondy (1974:45) elaborates on the theme of "wagelessness and survival without a job" as a creation of the black youth culture of resistance:

> (A) large number of black unemployed youth refuse to register with state agencies and support themselves by drawing sustenance and strength from the life of the community. They refuse the work that society allocates to them.... Their rejection of work is a rejection of the level to which schools have skilled them as labor power....

In contrast, the Jocks display much more willingness than their British counterparts to search for and acquire unskilled jobs. This may be so because first-generation Jocks in Canada perceive menial, unskilled labor as part-time and temporary employment only, and envisage moving on to better jobs when they graduate from school. However, their future relationship with the work force will likely be negatively influenced by their low level of educational and occupational preparation for the labor market.

SUMMARY AND CONCLUSION

To summarize, there is a wide gap between the Jocks' career aspirations and the vocational training they receive in school. Their lower level of training and certification at Lumberville put them at a distinct disadvantage to their higher-track peers when they compete for scarce jobs. It is quite likely then that the Jocks' menial, unskilled work that is now part-time and temporary will, in the near future, become full-time and permanent. This chapter has uncovered the importance of sports both to the Jocks' culture and to Lumberville's institutional structure. For the Jocks, sports serve three main functions: it helps in the formation of black culture and identity; it preserves machismo; and it is pursued as a viable channel for socioeconomic advancement. To the Jocks such identity formation is based primarily on the belief that blacks are superior to other racial groups in sports, and have such personal attributes as aptitude, physical characteristics, and personality dispositions to be outstanding athletes. This belief system was reinforced by researchers such as Ikulayo (1982) and others who suggest that racial differences in athletic performance may also be physiologically determined. Despite the debates surrounding such assessment of "black is best" (Kane, 1971), black students have cemented their identities around sports. Such an identity formation is helped along by socializing agents such as teachers and coaches, peers, and black models in the media.

Preoccupation with sports also provides the Jocks with some degree of machismo in a school setting where they are tracked to the lowest-level academic programs, and in a society where their manhood has been eroded by racial subordination. Their reluctance to participate in traditional female activities and "sissy games" is an indication of their strong need to preserve machismo. Willis's (1977: 153) thesis that British black male involvement in school sports may well be that they have "preserved a degree of machismo from the real and imputed degradation of their conditions." For the Jocks at Lumberville, sport involvement may be their way of regaining some of the social status lost because of their social and academic position in the institutional structure.

Finally, the Jocks turn to sports as a channel for social advancement after realizing that the conventional route through education is not always open to them. They preoccupy themselves acquiring and developing athletic skills and competencies that they think will win them scholarships to U.S. colleges. The Jocks expect such institutions to prepare them to become professional sportsmen such as those portrayed in the media.

Lumberville, on the other hand, utilized its sports program for institutional needs that are quite different from those of the Jocks. Publicly, sports bring recognition to the school and helps to build positive relations with its immediate community. At the more private level, sports function mainly as a social control mechanism, neutralizing black resistance to the rules and routines of the school. Capitalizing on the black students' cultivated interest in sports, the school establishes a marriage between sport participation and allegiance to school rules. Students must be in good standing behaviorally and academically to participate in organized school sports. For those black students who have aspirations of advancing academically at Lumberville but find the program is inadequate for fulfilling that dream, sports become an available and attractive alternative, cooling out the academic desires of such students, Solomon (1989) concludes (see table 1).

When we examine the function of sports for the Jocks and for Lumberville we realize that the academic needs of the Jocks are seriously compromised. With little or no interest in academic pursuits, the Jocks will end up controlling sports, an area of school life that unfortunately is marginal and inadequate for social advancement in Canadian society. In the end, we see Lumberville providing athletic opportunities in exchange for student acquiescence to official authority. Those at odds with the rules and regularities of the school are forced into an ambiguous and compromising relationship with the authority structure. Overt resistance is replaced by caged resentment and covert acts of defiance. So although Lumberville's authority structure was able to contain student resistance, domination is not complete. In the next chapter we examine some of the strategies the Jocks employ to extricate themselves from the institutional controls of Lumberville.

TABLE 1

School Sports
Cultural and Institutional Utility

Cultural Functions

•Builds black culture, cohesion, and identity
•Preserves machismo from degradation of conditions within school and community
•Perceived as channel for social advancement

Institutional Functions

•Brings recognition to school and community
•Serves as a social control mechanism
•Neutralizes black resistance to rules and routines
•Serves as cooling-out process for academic aspirants

CHAPTER 6

The School:
Contribution to Separatism

Educational theorists and researchers have described schools as "sorting machines" in which children are sorted, classified, and grouped according to their abilities, aptitudes, and needs. This selection process starts at an early age as Rist's (1970) research shows, and continues through to high school where students are tracked, instructed, and socialized according to their projected socioeconomic stations in life. A revealing feature of track level placement in multiracial schools is that students from racial minority groups and low socioeconomic status are more likely than others to be in the lowest academic tracks. Bowles and Gintis (1976) assert that such low-track programs are characterized by the learning of respect for authority, rule following, and direction taking. Oakes's (1982) exploration of this hypothesis supports the claim that track placement fosters the gradual separation of students along racial and social lines as they move through high school and into the workplace. This chapter describes two salient and interrelated features of schooling at Lumberville, its track allocation and its student control mechanisms. Are the Jocks' oppositional cultural forms in any way a response to these institutional structures? In what ways may these school structures contribute to the boys' own separatist culture? Here, we explore these themes.

THE SORTING MACHINE

Lumberville's admission policy is a part of a systemwide selection process that sorts and allocates students leaving the elementary schools into the following high school tracks: vocational track, occupational track; general academic track; and the advanced academic tracks for students who are university-bound. One unique feature of this allocation process is that the vocational track program such as Lumberville's is located separate and apart from the higher-tracks general and advanced level programs that are housed together. This stratification of knowledge may well contribute to the separatism, not only among levels of programs, but also among social class and racial groups, as will be shown later. In addition to the tracking that occurs among schools, there is considerable separation of students for instructional purposes within Lumberville. With the use of sorting tools such as tests, students are divided into three main groups: high, middle, and low, to facilitate instruction.

Working-class West Indian immigrant students are most likely candidates for programs such as Lumberville's. First, a large number arrive in Canada with little or no documentation of their past schooling and academic level of functioning. To determine class placement, academic achievement tests are given.[1] Some students fare poorly on such tests because test materials and testing procedures do not relate to their past learning experiences or their learning styles. Quite often, some of these students attended school irregularly in their country of origin, or had even dropped out of school entirely, and are therefore out of touch with the content and process of schooling. New and unfamiliar schooling experiences as well as social adjustment factors within the community and home all contribute to the students' poor response on standardized tests, and thus their qualification for placement at a low-track school such as Lumberville.

Some teachers, parents, and students are critical of placement procedures and the quality of the program that students receive at Lumberville.

> Teacher: To put them [West Indian immigrant students] in that school [Lumberville] a special test is done.... The test does not recognize any cultural factors that would cause a kid from, say, Jamaica, not to recognize a set of words. When they come to Canada, unless they are already familiar with Canadian vocabulary, it would be very hard for them to do well on these tests. People say that these tests have no cultural bias, but I think that they do. I administer them every year.... Some of the vocabulary in these tests, I don't know how they expect any immigrant from Jamaica to know their meanings...

For the parents of the Jocks in this study, they expected the school system to provide the optimum educational opportunities for their children. Their goal of migrating to Canada was for their children to achieve some measure of upward mobility through schooling. Ike's mother explained her reason for immigrating this way:

> I came because of the kids. It was so hard back home; so for them I have to fight to see if they can turn out to be something. Honestly, I don't have an education and I don't have a trade. I don't want my children to grow up the same way. That's the main reason I've got to try for them.

These parents' conception of high school education is based on the type in their homeland that prepares students for middle-class jobs and a chance at postsecondary education. Access to such education was limited to those who passed entrance examinations or those who could afford the direct cost. In Canada, the immigrant parents' frame of reference led them to expect the same or even more from a school system that they perceived as more advanced and sophisticated than that of their homeland. Access to high school education without entrance examinations or without direct cost gave the appearance of an open opportunity structure. The school system in Canada came under scrutiny only after parents realized that their children were not getting the types of education for the jobs of their choice, nor the academic credentials to move on to postsecondary education. Many of these parents claimed that at the time of their children's placement at Lumberville, they were not aware of its low-track status, nor did they understand the multitrack high school system in existence in Ontario. This claim was borne out in the following interview:

> PS: Were you aware of the type of high school program offered at Lumberville?
>
> Mitch's Mother: Not initially. I didn't know what the different levels meant until it was too late to do anything about Mitch's placement. I suspected something was wrong when his twin sister who attended the same elementary school as Mitch was promoted to another high school.
>
> PS: Did you know that the Lumberville program does not prepare its students for college or university?
>
> Mitch's Mother: I didn't know initially, but now I know.

A survey of parental perceptions and involvement within the Lumber Valley School district conducted by a parent advocacy group confirms, "Parents indicated they were unaware that the vocational and basic programs would exclude their children from attending postsecondary institutions, e.g. university."[2]

Lumberville has become popularly known as "Lumberdump" within the local community and the school district at large. It has been labeled a "dummy school" where rejects go as this teacher sees it: "A lot of people who teach in other schools feel that students at Lumberville are rejects.... Lumberville is going to be like a dumping ground for students." Black parents openly express disappointment and nonconfidence in the effectiveness of Lumberville's school program even to provide useful education for their children:

> Roy's Mother: What Roy is getting in that school [Lumberville] I would classify as training to work in a factory or in a restaurant; that's it! If he drops out of school and gets a trade, some company may give him a break and offer to train him...

> Mitch's Mother: Mitch is wasting his time at Lumberville. He doesn't
> know what will happen after he finishes grade twelve
> there.

As a result of this loss of confidence in Lumberville to help blacks realize their mobility goals, parents of the Jocks have started contesting feeder
schools' intentions to transfer more of their children to Lumberville. Here,
two parents relate their opposition to the school's allocation process.

> Ike's Mother: I have another thirteen-year-old daughter going to Bur-
> bank [feeder school] and they [school administration at
> Burbank] are pushing me so hard to transfer her into Lum-
> berville. And I said, "I don't care, I'm not signing the
> paper for her to go there. I have two going there already
> and that's it!" I saw kids that don't know as much [as her
> daughter] go to Lumberlea [Collegiate] and ended up
> attending Lumber [Community] College and pursuing a
> career in word processing. She wasn't very bright, but at
> least she went there [Lumberlea Collegiate]. I'm not
> going to send my daughter to Lumberville!

> Leroy's Mother: I have a younger son that they want to send over to Lum-
> berville. The teachers phoned me and said they were
> going to send him, and I said, "No way! He is going to
> stay right there at Burbank until he's old and grey." And
> now he passed his exams and he's supposed to go to Lum-
> berlea Collegiate.

Such parental responses show resistance to the school system's allocation practices of channeling siblings to education in a low-track school. Now
we examine the mechanisms employed by the school to regulate student
movement out of Lumberville and students' own creative response to such
regulations.

TRAPPED IN A "DUMMY" SCHOOL

One of the regularities of the Lumberville school program is its annual promotion of students to Eastway, a higher-track school. Only students who
have met the necessary academic and behavior expectations of their teachers
are sponsored. This process had been the officially accepted route out of
Lumberville. Over the years, however, the number of students sponsored to
Eastway decreased considerably as a teacher acknowledges, "Traditionally,
there has been forty to fifty kids who have gone to Eastway every year. That
number has decreased somewhat, one-eighth of this number goes to Eastway
these days."

There are two possible explanations for this marked decrease. Officially, Lumberville offers a full secondary school diploma program [following the upgrading of its status from a vocational to occupational]; therefore students do not need to be promoted to another school with a similar level program. The second factor that puts immense constraints on teacher sponsorship of students and interschool mobility is the effect of declining enrollment on the maintenance of teachers' jobs. There is a strong belief among Lumberville's teachers that if too many students are sponsored to Eastway, the pupil-teacher ratio at Lumberville would be thrown off balance. In a school system already experiencing declining enrollment, staff reduction at Lumberville would be an inevitable outcome of a large promotion of students to Eastway. To maintain a viable pupil-teacher ratio and secure their jobs, teachers have responded on two fronts. First, feedback from students indicated that teachers have counseled them privately that the shop programs at Eastway are no better than those at Lumberville, and it would be unwise to accept promotions there.

[In a group discussion]

> Byron: I could have gone to Eastway but a lot of people told me that the program there is not as good as Lumberville's.

> Garfield: I have been recommended for Eastway but I said no. It's the same thing as Lumberville's, really. It's just more of a trade, that's all. From what I hear from the Lumberville teachers, they [Eastway] don't pay much attention [to students] as they do here at Lumberville. And the classes there are really big, something like twenty-five students.

> PS: So the teachers at Lumberville are not pushing Eastway that much, then?

> Garfield: Oh no, not really.

Despite the teachers' denigration of the Eastway's school programs, the students and the community at large still perceive Lumberville as the "dummy school," an image that will not quickly disappear with the change of status from a vocational to an occupational school. Furthermore, school administrators admitted that promotion to Eastway would expose the student to a wider variety of shops and "open doors to more vocational opportunities" than Lumberville would. The common understanding among staff is that there is a difference: "Eastway is high basic. The program we [Lumberville] offer, at this time, is slightly lower." Contradictory messages have emerged on these accounts. The clarifications students claim they receive from the staff conflict greatly with the information communicated to teachers by the administration.

The second response by teachers to maintain a viable pupil-teacher ratio at Lumberville is to reduce the number of students they sponsor to Eastway annually. A teacher explained:

> The rate at which we now send students out to Eastway is very slow. Each member of staff wants to have a class to teach, and one has to keep up her class size. You must keep even one bright student to show you are teaching something…especially if the child is not very assertive, one that will not ask, "Why am I staying here? I've got my marks. I did my work; it is not fair."

Some teachers are morally opposed to the practice of "holding students back" in order to maintain a stable pupil-teacher ratio.

> Teacher: There is a feeling within the school although I don't agree with it. My colleagues are asking, "Why should we be sending these kids to Eastway when we are cutting our own throats? We should be hanging on to every kid we can, so we can hang on to every teacher we can." Well, that's playing the numbers game with kids' education. If a kid is capable of a higher level of functioning, which means he is an Eastway candidate, then I say, send him, and let the chips fall where they may…. We are not in the business of maintaining our jobs. We are in the business of educating kids…. There are people at Lumberville who are upset by my ideas, because when it comes to education, I'm a bit of an idealist.

Despite some teachers' supportive stances on student sponsorship, the unwritten rule among teachers at Lumberville appears to be: "don't cut your own throats," and the necessity of "holding students back" to maintain the staff complement remains in vogue. This has become dysfunctional to the educational mobility of black students there. It is revealing that such external constraints as declining student enrollment and its effects on teachers' job security mediate sponsorship and program accessibility. It is interesting that at Lumberville teachers' middle-class jobs have become dependent on their assessment and maintenance of black, working-class students as low functioning.

"ESCAPE FROM LUMBERDUMP"

Because a stream of student promotions to higher-track schools has been reduced over the years to a trickle, the Jocks and their parents have explored alternative "underground" routes out of Lumberville, in search of better schooling.

> Teacher: Students can get there (Eastway) without recommendation, provided their parents go to the Board of Education and say, "I want my child to attend Eastway." And this has happened…. But strangely enough, this has not happened with the kids [Jocks] we are talking about. I know of three or four [who were able to transfer to Eastway], but these are not black kids in the athletic program at all.

School administrators reiterated that students do have "the right to fail"; that is, to transfer to a higher-track and a more difficult program without the recommendation of school personnel and running the risk of failing. There is also a placement appeal procedure that dissatisfied parents are entitled to use, but the process is so complicated and drawn out that no parent has bothered to use it.

The large majority of black parents have not gone the institutional route but have left it up to the students themselves to design their own "exit routes."

> Ike: Staying at Lumberville for grade twelve means I'd have to go back there next year again. I wouldn't want to do that; I'd be there six years and people would be laughing in my face.... I'm trying to go to Eastway next year. If I stay at Lumberville they wouldn't promote me to Eastway.

> Ike's Mother: I agree with Ike for getting a transfer because he is at Lumberville for so many years and was beginning to get bored. He wants to go into a training program at Eastway and he feels that he wouldn't be able to get there from Lumberville.

Ike went about planning his exit route this way (see figure 3): Although his ultimate destination was Eastway, his first step was to apply for an interdistrict transfer and register at Yorkville, a school outside his district's jurisdiction. From Yorkville his application to Eastway for the upcoming school year would be processed as if Ike were a new student moving into the Lumber Valley school district for the first time.

Over the years this route has become well developed and the Jocks speak knowledgeably of others who have used this "underground" route successfully. Other "exit routes" were revealed in a group discussion:

> Ike: This other girl who was at Lumberville last year got a transfer to Yorkville. Now Yorkville told her she's too smart and promoted her to York Forest [a collegiate that offers programs one to two tracks higher than Eastway and two to three levels higher than Lumberville]. Lumberville wouldn't send her to Eastway because they didn't think she had enough brains to go there. If she didn't transfer to Yorkville she would still be at Lumberville.

> Roy: My sister used to go to Lumberville four years ago and they [teachers] told her she was not smart enough to go to Eastway. So my Mom sent her down to Eastway and now she is too smart for Eastway. She is going to Lumberlea Collegiate in a grade twelve program.

> PS: Are you returning to Lumberville after the holidays?

> Roy: No. They can't give me anything to go back there. I was supposed to go to Eastway, but I changed my mind.

> PS: So what other school are you thinking of?

Roy: I want to transfer to York Park [in another school district]; that's the only school around.

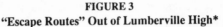

FIGURE 3
"Escape Routes" Out of Lumberville High*

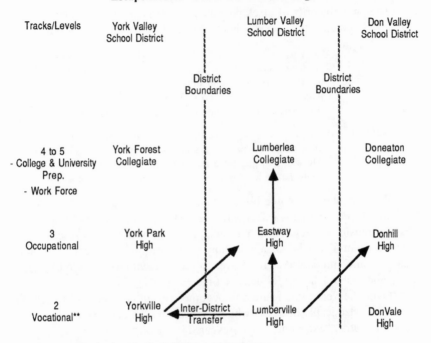

Tracks/Levels	York Valley School District		Lumber Valley School District		Don Valley School District
		District Boundaries		District Boundaries	
4 to 5 - College & University Prep. - Work Force	York Forest Collegiate		Lumberlea Collegiate		Doneaton Collegiate
3 Occupational	York Park High		Eastway High		Donhill High
2 Vocational**	Yorkville High	Inter-District Transfer	Lumberville High		DonVale High

* All names of schools and school districts are pseudonyms.

** The "Level 2" designation was eliminated from use in the Ontario Ministry of Education circular, Ontario Schools: Intermediate and Senior Divisions (OSIS) 1984.

In a time of decreasing enrollment and the increasing need for job security among teachers, schools within the Metropolitan Toronto school districts increasingly compete for scarce students. Here, a Lumberville teacher relates the ease with which student transfers are affected, "Because of declining enrollment other schools are willing to take the kids carte blanche, with no questions asked. They are even telling kids how to go about getting an interborough transfer. They are quite happy to get kids so that they may keep their enrollment up; while on the other side of the coin, our school is unhappy about the loss of enrollment."

Student-initiated transfers are not always accomplished without obstacles. While pursuing the Lumberville–Yorkville–Eastway route, students who do not remain at Yorkville long enough to accumulate credentials are asked to provide reports from previous schools. It is at this juncture that the

Lumberville authorities are least cooperative, blocking student transfers to their desired schools.

> PS: Is the staff supportive of students who leave Lumberville without their recommendation?

> Teacher: No. Those who leave tend to come back for some kind of reference. Lumberville's recommendations are not always based on academic ability, but also on behavior suitability.

From these accounts it is evident that students' unilateral transfers to escape the regularities of Lumberville are accomplished only with great inconvenience and sacrifice. They initiate the processing of documents necessary for transfer—for example, interdistrict transfers and recommendations—and commit themselves to commute long distances with additional expenditure for transportation to out-of-district schools. These sacrifices indicate the Jocks' commitment to the ideology of achievement through schooling, but not the Lumberville schooling that they perceived as "leading nowhere."

HOW STAFF RULE

Closely related to the student selection and allocation mechanism in place at Lumberville is its authority structure. Such a structure embraces not only explicit codes of behavior, but the more subtle student control techniques implicit in its reward system.

> As a community, Lumberville has clear expectations of desirable behavior. The reasons for such expectations, as well as the possible consequences of misbehavior are listed below. The code of behavior reflects the concern that the staff, students, and parents have for the security and well being of everyone at Lumberville. (Code of Behavior, Lumberville High)

The code outlines such expected behaviors as: regular attendance, punctuality, respect for authority, respect for others, respect for property, freedom from the influence of alcohol or drugs, and proper classroom behavior. For each of these the "reasons for the expectations" and the "consequences of misbehavior" are precisely stated. Upon comparison, Lumberville's code of behavior resembles that of any other high school within the school district. It is, rather, staff interpretation and enforcement of these rules, and the imposition of "unwritten" rules, that are the primary source of conflict between staff and students. For example, the dress code states that clothing must be appropriate for an institution of learning. Teachers' interpretation of this code prohibits the wearing of hats in school, posing a problem for subcultural groups that wear brightly colored toques both as a "cover-up" for their unkempt hair, and as a style of dress popular among black boys who embrace the Rasta culture. Another code states that "Students involved in fights on school property or on a school-sponsored activity face suspension from school." This code causes overzealous teachers to view with suspicion any physical encounter between students. It is not uncommon to see Jocks locked in physical struggles in classrooms, in hallways, or on the playground. To the culturally unknowledgeable such encounters may be interpreted as a fight in progress. But in the culture of the Jocks, this interactional style is nonmalicious and may even be an act of comradeship.

Yet other rules control the students' space and time within the school. Teachers on duty in the corridors, the cafeteria, and the gymnasium are vigilant in their enforcement of school rules, intercepting and punishing violators. Prior to the start of classes, teachers straddle the line between their classroom and the corridors keeping an eye on both fronts. Another form of teacher control over students' time and space involves the use of "time sheets" to record and monitor student absence from the classroom for such reasons as to go to the washroom, or to see other teachers. Students must "sign out" when they leave the classroom, and "sign in" upon their return.

While some teachers are nontransactional with students in enforcing school rules, others utilize brief discussion sessions for clarifying institutional behavior. Here, the Jocks discuss problems they encountered with staff and students around the school. For example, Weston wanted to know if teachers have the right to interfere with his private business. "I'm walking along the hallway with Pam [girlfriend], right? I put my arm around her. The guy [teacher] said, 'Leave the girl alone.' I said to him, 'Hold on, it's none of your business if I want to put my hand around her...'" The institutional response to this altercation was that staff does have the right to question hallway behavior and to follow school policy.

Reprimand is probably the least severe consequence for undesirable behavior. This ranges from the teacher casting a reprimanding eye in the direction of violators, writing "4:00 D" [detention until 4 p.m. after the 3:05 p.m. school dismissal] on the chalkboard, to sending offending students to the school office for punishment.

[In an interview on punishments]

> PS: Students think they are automatically removed from school sport teams if they are sent to the school office for disciplinary action.

> Teacher: They are probably talking about me, but it's not really that bad, although they'd like to give that impression.... Sometimes you have to get downright nasty and angry with them to shake them up.... Even when you are coaching there has to be discipline.

Detentions and suspensions are two closely linked consequences used by staff to control student behavior. The school statistics show that over 150 suspensions lasting from three to five days are handed out annually. School administrators are convinced that suspensions are very effective in controlling behavior since students have no social life outside the school and therefore prefer to be in school. The staff maintains a rigid monitoring system to ensure that students on detention or suspension do not gain access to regular classes until they have served their consequences. Students such as Weston rebel against school rules and the consequences for breaking them:

> Some school rules are no good, man! If you are late for school and he [V.P.] gives you an "8:15" [detention] and if you miss it, the guy doubles it. If you don't show up the following day (to serve the detention), he suspends you. The guy suspends for nothing; just like that, suspend!

The police are an integral cog in the school's student control mechanism. Their essential functions are to respond to emergency situations such as fights, to be on duty at special school functions, to investigate and apprehend trespassers and troublemakers on school property, and to be a symbol of authority to uncooperative and oppositional students. The Jocks resent their threatening presence and their use by the administration to maintain the authority structure.

[Group Discussion]

> Boyd: For every little thing the V.P. calls the police. Everything that happens, he calls the police. Say he tells you to leave the school building on suspension and you try to talk to him, he threatens to call the police to remove you. He doesn't even want to hear what you want to say.
>
> PS: Why would they want to suspend you in the first place?
>
> Boyd: They said I broke their window. But I didn't break the school window.
>
> PS: What did they do about it?
>
> Boyd: They phoned the police on me. That's why I wanted to leave this school so bad.
>
> PS: Did the police talk to you?
>
> Boyd: Yes, they came to my house.
>
> PS: Did you have to pay, or were you charged?
>
> Boyd: No, 'cause they know I didn't do it.
>
> PS: What are some of the reasons why cops are called to the school?
>
> Weston: Suppose he [V.P.] finds out them guys at the school smoke [marijuana], he calls the cops to search their locker. Sometimes the guys say "no" because they [police] don't have no search warrant.... If he [V.P.] is suspicious, he calls you down to the office and questions you, and then he says, "I'm going to call the cops."

The Jocks strongly believe that the school photographs that are taken yearly are used jointly by the school authorities and the police for the identification of "wrongdoers." This certainly is the belief of at least some of the Jocks, from an individual interview on police intervention:

Weston: Certain times of the year some guy comes to the school and takes your picture, right? They make you go back and take a next set of pictures, and you *have* to take them. And they [school authorities] put them in this file. And then when somebody gets into trouble, they call the cop, and the cop goes through the file. When they see your picture, they give the cop everything.

PS: These pictures, how often are they taken, once a year?

Weston: Yes, and they keep it in this file, and they send some to the cops. When you get in trouble they look through the file and if they recognize your picture they phone him [V.P.] and he tells them yes, and they [police] come over for it. Every time you see the cops up there [at the school].

In addition to the institutional use of the police for student surveillance, the police are readily available to intervene in fights among students and altercations between students and staff. At such interventions the police become a target of student hostility. Police participation in system maintenance is evident in cases of locker break-ins and vandalism, where their involvement is to investigate and to apprehend. In a less urgent but nonetheless conspicuous role, police presence is used as a symbol of authority at special functions and events. Uniformed, armed officers are on duty at school dances, graduation ceremonies, open house programs, and sport events.

The use of the police as a control agent in schools is not an entirely new practice. Under the guise of "community relations," direct control is exerted by the police in British multiracial schools. Carby (1982:207) comments:

The police with the support of the teaching staff, will seek to assist within the schools in developing law abiding young people. The construction of the 'fear' of crime by black youth is used as a justification to police them in schools. Policing them in the classroom also aids with identifying and monitoring black youth on the streets.

It is noteworthy that this extreme form of control over students' time and space, buttressed by police intervention, is a feature of schools, both in Britain and Canada, with a large proportion of black youth.

In addition to the more overt control techniques such as detentions, suspensions, and police interventions, teachers utilize indirect approaches to maintain student control. The roles and responsibilities of Student Council members are defined, not by the student body that elected them, or by the councillors themselves, but by the school staff. Mitch, while president of the Student Council, claimed his position was constantly undermined by the staff supervisor. He claimed that the more pro-establishment vice president was given a higher profile within the school community, and was authorized by the staff to make announcements on the public address system and represent the student body at school district meetings. These are traditionally the functions of the president. Staff not only dictated the councillors' roles and responsibilities, but publicly discredited members who were perceived as counterschool, and a threat to the authority structure of the school. Mitch, who claims he was forced to resign the presidency because of staff intervention, recalls one such incident:

> Mitch:　I heard Miss Galt on the announcements saying that Mitch couldn't handle the work [presidency]. I don't know why she said I couldn't handle the work because there wasn't any work for me to handle.... As I walked through the halls all the Student Council members were saying, "Did you hear how Miss Galt put you down, man!"

Teachers exercise rigid control over school-sponsored social activities. Male teachers perform an active gatekeeping role, blocking the entry of students on suspension and other unwelcome persons to the school. Another effective measure of control employed by the staff is restricting the flow of information to students about upcoming social events. This control technique is based on the belief that students' anticipation of planned social events increases their subcultural behaviors leading up to and at the time of the event.

REWARDS AS CONTROL

Lumberville's reward system is the other dimension of its student control strategy. This system is reflected in the school's annual commencement presentations. Here, rewards for proschool behaviors are given equal importance to those for academic achievement. Qualifications for some of these awards, explained a school administrator, are based on such social qualities as "good influence on the school community," "good, faithful behavior in school," "good behavior," and "positive attitude."

Athletic awards to students who have contributed to the Lumberville sports program are presented at annual "Recognition Banquets." Here, special athletic skills development awards as well as the more general awards for representing the school in sports are given to a large number of students each year (forty-one in 1983, thirty-four in 1984). Since qualifications to play on school teams are excellent behavior, satisfactory progress in academic work, and good attendance, conformity to school norms and values are therefore implicitly rewarded in these athletic presentations. In addition to the formal reward structure of Lumberville, individual staff members set their own arbitrary standards by which they reward students for proschool behaviors. By giving the Jocks the privilege of leaving classes early or missing them altogether to participate in athletic events, teachers expect reciprocity and adherence to conformist behaviors.

SUMMARY AND CONCLUSION

This chapter describes two institutional features of Lumberville that contribute to student alienation from the mainstream. First, allocating students to the lowest academic track and isolating them in a setting popularly known as "Lumberdump" not only restrict educational opportunities for these students but segregate them socially from students in the academic mainstream. Within Lumberville, a further sorting of students for instructional purposes has the effect of grouping at the bottom of the academic hierarchy many of the recently arrived West Indian immigrants. Researchers such as Rosenbaum (1976), Oakes (1982), and McLaren (1986) view such sorting and differential socialization of students as reflective of the racial and social divisions in society. They argue that working-class and minority groups occupy the lowest rung in a hierarchical social and economic system and their children are being schooled to follow in their parents' footsteps. Realizing that the cards are stacked against them at Lumberville, the Jocks embarked on a sophisticated system of departure in search of better schooling. The institution's response to such an unauthorized exodus of students was to make transfers even more difficult. These competing interests inevitably led to conflict and divisiveness between the school on the one hand and the students and their parents on the other.

The second institutional mechanism that contributes to student alienation is its use of rules and rewards to achieve conformity. Students such as the Jocks perceive Lumberville's codes of behavior as restrictive to their rights to dress, and congregate, interact, and communicate in a style they claim is culturally befitting. The school's top-down imposition of control, bolstered by external forces such as the police, demanded student conformity but got instead student resistance, alienation, and distance. Chapter 7 examines some of the outcomes of conflict between the authority structure of the school and the lived culture of the Jocks.

CHAPTER 7

When Structure and Culture Collide: The Outcome of Schooling

The previous chapter provided a description of the allocation mechanisms employed by a school system in general, and Lumberville High more specifically, to sort students into multilevel tracks for instruction and socialization. This ethnography captured the oppositional responses of students and their parents to such tracking when they realized the limitations of such a program to the achievement of their life objectives. In this chapter we analyze the long-term effects of Lumberville's sorting mechanism on the future of the Jocks as a working-class, racial minority within Canada's socioeconomic structure. What opportunities will they have in a work force that prefers higher-track, dominant-group workers? Does "escaping" Lumberville for other schools provide the Jocks any real opportunity for better education, or is this escape more of a political act of resistance? Realizing that schooling at Lumberville does not support their aspirations, the Jocks embarked upon alternative strategies such as school sports. Are the Jocks' chances of "making it" even more remote because they have chosen sports, an area where the odds of success are too great? Here, we move beyond its in-school cultural and institutional functions and argue that curricular sports may well contribute to the reproduction of black marginality in Canadian society.

Finally, we locate the Jocks' ethnospecific culture of resistance within a structural-culturalist theoretical framework and show how its conflictual relationship with the authority structure of the school moves into a negative spiral that contributes to black separation and alienation from mainstream culture. How does this study contribute to the theories of race and resistance? Here, we compare the findings of research on the black culture of resistance in Britain and the United States with that of the somewhat ethnically and generationally different West Indian immigrants in Canada. Does their response to the opportunity structure and the racial climate in Canada contribute to the theory of black resistance in a white mainstream structure? To conclude, I express the concern of the West Indian community that its differential commitment to ethnic identity may lead to a future polarization of blacks in Canadian society.

THE REPRODUCTIVE EFFECTS OF TRACKING

The existence of a multitrack system in Ontario high schools and a further internal sorting mechanism within schools such as Lumberville High have stratified the Jocks to the very bottom of the educational opportunity structure. Realizing that such low-track programs do not prepare students for careers of their choosing the Jocks have built in reality-based alternatives such as being an office cleaner instead of a professional hockey player, or a weight lifter instead of an attorney. Such a lowering of aspirations is certainly in keeping with Lumberville's expressed objectives of preparing students for the workplace, and not for college to "study attorney." Track placement, therefore, becomes a very powerful determinant of the interrelated schooling process and outcome. In the process of schooling, researchers studying attrition in Ontario high schools have established that students from lower academic tracks drop out of school at a far greater rate than those in higher tracks (Radwanski 1988). Black students who are disproportionately tracked to low-level programs become potential candidates for attrition. The fact that they are less likely than their white peers to terminate in the early years of their high school career suggests that black students still hold a strong belief in schooling as their only vehicle for social advancement.

With regards to the outcome of schooling, Larter, Cheng, and Wright's (1980:16) research on tracking in Metropolitan Toronto and other Ontario school jurisdictions highlights the relationship between the quality of vocational preparation, the level of placement in the labor force hierarchy, and the subsequent wages disparities:

> Given the different types of training students receive in the different streams, it is not surprising to find that the types of jobs held vary from unskilled and semi-skilled low paying jobs such as janitor, waiter, taxi driver, sales clerk and factory worker for levels two and three [vocational & occupational] students to more skilled, better paying jobs such as commercial artist, bookkeeper and auto mechanic for levels four and five [academic and university prep] students.

Harvey's (1980) study confirms the occupational status and wage differences between graduates of the two lower tracks. Graduates of the vocational track were found to be employed mainly in the service sector, while those of the occupational track were in the industrial sector and earned a higher wage. Closely linked to track placement are employment patterns. School leavers, whether graduates or dropouts, from higher tracks have a higher rate of employment than their lower-track counterparts who tend to be unemployed for long periods of time after leaving school. Both Harvey and Larter found that for part-time and summer jobs, employers favor students from the higher-track programs. Joblessness and wagelessness among low-track school leavers such as Lumberville's, then, are sometimes triggered by a nonschool factor: employer preferences in the labor market. With the relative worthlessness of the credentials offered at Lumberville, the Jocks cannot compete with the qualifications of higher-track graduates.

A second nonschool factor that will impede the Jocks relates to the level of employer discrimination against racial minorities in the Toronto job market. As we have seen in chapter 2, substantial employment barriers severely limit the job opportunities of the uneducated, unqualified, and unskilled black school leavers. Employers with a preference for white workers not only deny blacks equal access to job opportunities, but they also restrict the promotions and earning power of blacks to levels below those of their counterparts. Consequently, the match between the aspirations and occupational reality of blacks remains remote. In reality, the Jocks' job stations after school, on weekends, and during the holiday breaks—loading trucks, washing dishes, cleaning offices, distributing flyers, and performing a variety of other unskilled tasks—will likely be their permanent occupations in life.

Tracking and employers' racial preferences in the labor market have combined to maintain and reproduce the black working class at the lower echelons of Canada's socioeconomic hierarchy. Students such as the Jocks will be no further ahead of their immigrant parents who already occupy a similarly low status. This preservation of entrance status calls into question the classical model of immigrant assimilation which theorizes that most immigrants enter a socioeconomic system at the lowest level and become upwardly mobile by the next generation. For the West Indian, race may well be a major factor in the immobility of their entrance status. Li's (1978:31) study of ethnic immigrants in Toronto found that "inequality persists despite adjustments for intergroup differences in social origin, education and prior achieved occupational status." For the children of these groups, factors such as schooling must be implicated as a variable in the reproduction of low socioeconomic status. But have the Jocks passively accepted the station in life defined by their schooling at Lumberville?

SCHOOL HOPPING AND SPORTS: LIBERATING OR REPRODUCTIVE?

The Jocks' response to their schooling at Lumberville has contradicted the conventional view of working-class students as passive objects of educational and occupational selection. Individual or group-motivated transfers to higher-track schools that will expose them to better education and life opportunities may be viewed as a progressive rather than reproductive element of the group's culture. The Jocks have become active agents engaged in a struggle to break the reproductive effect of the school program to which they were allocated. "Escaping" from Lumberville is emancipatory to a group of boys who have rejected the subordinate economic roles defined by the school they attend. School transfers by the Jocks and other black students at Lumberville may be compared to job hopping of black school graduates in Britain: both groups can prove to themselves and to one another that they are discontented with the position the schools have prescribed for them in the social structure. By not settling in dead-end situations, Roberts, Duggan, and Noble (1983:201) conclude, "Black youth are more likely to 'solve' their predicaments ideologically without surrendering their aspirations." While "escapism" is a liberating act determined to break away from a school curriculum that will not improve the Jock's social class position in Canadian society, it may also be viewed as an act of resistance, challenging the structural regularities of the school. Fine's (1982) study of high school dropouts in New York City found that these students were not the victims of "learned helplessness" as previously thought, but were the most critical and politically astute students. Fine (1982:6) further found that: "(I)t was the dropouts who were most likely to identify injustice in their social lives and at school, and were most ready to correct injustices by criticizing or challenging a teacher."

The Jocks' process of planning and effecting transfers to higher-track schools without the support and recommendation of Lumberville may be viewed as a political act designed to break a schooling process they abhor. While "exiting" removes students from politically and socially transforming the school they are leaving, they cannot be faulted for exploring emancipatory education elsewhere. It is important to note that by "escaping" to other schools, instead of dropping out, the Jocks are affirming their desire for a "better" education. It is the process and quality of schooling at Lumberville that they reject. Throughout the study, the Jocks perceived school hopping as a search for a better school environment that would provide the opportunity to realize their potential in athletics. At Lumberville they had utilized sports primarily to cement black culture and identity, to preserve some degree of machismo, and most importantly, to provide a channel for social advancement. Such a complete reliance on athletics to achieve these social and cultural objectives left little room for the more conventional academic curricula to work for the Jocks. With the avenues of advancement diverted away from the pursuit of academic credentials, the Jocks invest valuable instructional and recreational time perfecting their athletic skills with the expectation that future benefits will accrue. But the available evidence suggests that their chances are rather remote. In the United States and Britain, for the thousands of high school athletes who move into postsecondary institutions each year, only a few gain entry to the ranks of professional sportsmen and benefit financially from careers in athletics. This means that for the vast majority who had pursued school sports at the expense of the mainstream curriculum, life without sport is likely to be economically and socially marginal. For the working-class racial minorities such as the Jocks, school sports have simply reinforced their social and economic marginality. For this immigrant group, sports have not provided a channel for the upward social mobility they sought. Leaman and Carrington (1985:214) conclude that beyond the low and unstable income and low social status, "marginality is also a matter of one's life being in some ways at the disposal of others and not really under one's own control...."

It appears then that whether sports are pursued at Lumberville or at higher-track schools, their potential for socioeconomic benefits is very limited. Conversely, when school transfers are effected for academic reasons, there is a higher probability that long-term benefits will accrue. This was evident from reports on the number of female students who transferred from Lumberville for academic reasons and completed successfully higher-track academic programs before moving on to post secondary education. From these findings we can conclude that transfers to higher-track schools for academic pursuits can prove emancipatory and be upwardly mobile for working-class immigrant students. School hopping for athletic reasons, on the other hand, tends to reproduce the marginal status of the black working class in Canadian society.

WHEN STRUCTURE AND CULTURE COLLIDE

Throughout this study we have followed the conflictual relationship between the authority structure of Lumberville and the cultural practices of the Jocks. Let us now predict some of the possible outcomes of such a conflict. At the outset of this adversarial relationship is a school structure with a low-track curriculum, dominant-group norms and values, explicit top-down school policies, and codes of conduct that emphasize subordination to authority. Within such a setting we find a group of West Indian immigrant students whose distinct ethno-racial, linguistic, and cultural characteristics have thrusted them into conflict with the regularities of the school. Protecting school norms and values was often achieved at the expense of subordinating or devaluing the students' cultural forms. This brings into existence two opposing frames of reference. As an act of resistance against the institutional rules and routines that restrict their freedom, the Jocks respond with ethnospecific forms of behavior, often disguising subcultural activities as legitimate primary cultural behavior. Such acts of defiance include a language of resistance that extends beyond dialect to include double-talk and profanity;

slamming down dominoes to annoy the staff but defending such behavior as a cultural practice in a multicultural society. The teachers' inability to comprehend and to respond effectively to such oppositional cultural forms drive them to evoke authoritarian measures to maintain control. The Jocks' challenge to such arbitrary authoritarianism simply escalates this spiralling interaction, with structure and culture fueling each other. As this negative spiral intensifies, the Jocks become more alienated from the dominant group, and their educational opportunities become more restricted (see figure 4). Short and long-term suspensions from academic instruction, negative evaluation of nonconformist students, and the withdrawal of sponsorship to higher-track schools are some consequences. For those uncooperative students who circumvent the sponsorship routine and transfer to other schools unilaterally, positive testimonials are withheld.

FIGURE 4
When Structure and Culture Collide:
The Creation of Separatism

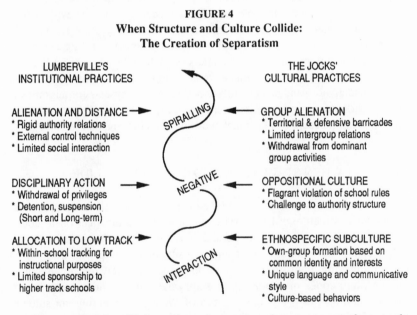

Entry to Lumberville's work-study program that exposes students to the world of work while still at school excludes those who do not embrace the school's norms, values, and expectations. Only students who demonstrate traits such as punctuality, good attendance, and reliability "need apply." Those whose subcultural behaviors challenge the authority structure of the school jeopardize their chances and are not given the opportunity to participate in these programs of transition from school to work. Gilmore's (1985) U.S. study of school resistance, attitude, and access to literacy, points to similar gatekeeping enterprises by teachers who deny children full access to education because of their nonalignment with the prevailing ethos of the school.

So in a school where a dialectical relationship exists between nonconformity to school regularities on the one hand, and a group's need for academic advancement on the other, the social power that teachers wield serves to depress or restrict the educational attainment of such a nonconformist group. Driver's (1977) research on the academic achievement of black students in a British school relates the extent to which students' classroom behaviors influence their teachers' educational judgement of them. He (pp. 356–357) describes the critical and problematic nature of teachers' assessments:

> The relative frequency of such classroom situations as these [conflicts] led the majority of teachers to make critical judgements of those West Indian pupils whom they considered "difficult".... In such a context as this, teachers were called upon to assess the abilities and achievements of pupils in their charge. Not only did teachers award marks and grades which were summarized in school report cards to parents, but they made recommendations upon which pupils were allocated to three sets or streams.

Because track allotment is such a powerful schooling process that determines academic futures and life chances, the long-term impact of student behaviors on teachers' educational judgements cannot be underestimated. The Lumberville data support Driver's position: it is not only the Jocks' oppositional culture that depresses their educational opportunities in school, but also their teachers' response to the culture. Consequently, when these black, working-class students end up in subordinate economic roles in society, the school cannot be absolved of the responsibility for this reproduction of the social order.

This conclusion moves beyond Willis's (1977) explanation that puts little weight on the educational institution itself for the successful reproduction of the class structure. At Lumberville, the top-down explicit school policies backed up by the teachers' implicit classroom codes have enormous importance in legitimizing the structuralist account of schooling. Teachers exercise control over student progress by distributing knowledge and rewards on the basis of student willingness to acquiesce to school authority. This points to the existence at Lumberville of the basic teaching paradigm which severely limits the educational opportunities of students who are oppositional.

The structure of authority relations within Lumberville has implications for interactions between control agents in the Canadian society and black working-class youth such as the Jocks. The authority structure of the school and the Jocks' response to it have set the stage for the polarization of the dominant authoritarian on the one hand and subordinate, oppositional positions on the other. This relationship will no doubt be reproduced in the workplace as the authority of employers runs into conflict with the youths' culture and aspirations. Beyond the social system of the school the theme of separation is likely to continue as a dominant feature of black life as they move into the world of work. This continuity will definitely be aided by the limited social interaction among different racial and cultural groups already there. In their study of the Toronto workplace, Billingsley and Muszynski (1985) found that language and communication patterns have a negative impact on intergroup social relations. Employers admitted: "We know we have a language problem here; the ethnic whites speak only Portuguese or Italian, the blacks speak their own island dialect. Nobody can understand each other!" (p.63).

In Britain, researchers found a substantial school-to-work continuity of black cultural forms and a widening of black and white relationships upon entry into employment. Given the climate of alienation already in existence in the Toronto labor market for which the Jocks are destined, and the Jocks' own impulse to separate along cultural lines, an adverse long-term intergroup social relationship appears to be entrenched at least for the next generation.

Finally, authority relations will likely be reproduced within the Jocks' community as the police, brought into the school as a control agent, become the main antagonists of black youth as they struggle for identity and self-formation in Canadian society. With black subcultural activities already bordering on delinquency within some of their ethnic enclaves, the police utilize the school-community link to identify and monitor black youth, a situation that is a source of concern in British schools (Carby, 1982). It is this intensive monitoring of "black life" that breathes antagonism between whites and blacks, between authority and the disempowered, and between dominant and marginalized cultures.

Given the impact of the collision between school structures and student cultures, how does the process of schooling at Lumberville relate to the theory of domination and resistance? Locating this study wholly within the structuralist's or the culturalist's explanation of schooling is problematic. The structuralist's criticism of schooling rightly identifies the powerful economic, political, and ideological forces in society that influence the schooling of subordinate groups. Their shortcoming is the perception of students simply as role-bearers with the powerful structural forces of the institution manipulating their consciousness and preparing them to take "their place" in a socioeconomic structure. As we critique the dominant institutional practices of Lumberville we become cognizant of its power to shape the futures of students who acquiesce to its domination. But the Jocks in this study did not submit to such domination; they exercised relative autonomy, relying on ethnospecific resources as tools of resistance. They devised creative strategies to escape from the futures that are determined by schooling at Lumberville. The weakness of structuralism is that it attaches little significance to any form of struggle and opposition to dominant institutional practices. This Lumberville study has highlighted the weakness in the structuralist's traditional view of schooling.

The culturalist's perspective, on the other hand, focuses on self-creation and the relative autonomy of cultural and subordinate groups within settings such as schools. This perspective was evident in the study of the Jocks and the cultural ammunition they displayed in their interaction with Lumberville's authority structure. One of the weaknesses of culturalism is its tendency to underrate the impact of institutional structures on the schooling process. As we have seen, in a rigidly tracked school such as Lumberville where program placement is reflective of the students' social class and, to some extent, racial and ethnic background, there is the tendency for its formal curriculum and its institutional routines to prepare students for specific slots in a stratified work force. The power of school structures to determine students' futures cannot be underestimated. A coherent, integrative perspective would not only capture the solo effect of structure and culture on the process and outcome of schooling, but would also highlight the dialectical relationships that exist between them. As we have seen at Lumberville, conflicts between the Jocks and the school's authority structure led to academic and social marginalization within the school community. This will undoubtedly translate into socioeconomic marginalization within the larger Canadian society.

A new integrative perspective would acknowledge the potential for structure and culture to assume a less rigid and more accommodative posture. Such a conciliatory posture leads to institutional structures that are more equitable and democratic, and student cultures that are less oppositional and subcultural. So instead of entering into negative spirals that are counterproductive to academic advancement, students and teachers will forge a new relationship that is conducive to progressive pedagogy. There has to be honest discourse about how and why sociopolitical forces within the wider society affect subordinate groups within schools, and how these disadvantaged groups may strategize to overcome subordination. Chapter 8 suggests starting points for reducing the negative impact of structure and culture.

RACE AND RESISTANCE: AN EXPANDED MODEL

The study of resistance to the reproduction of racial and ethnic inequality has been criticized by theorists such as Giroux (1983a, 1983b) and Fernandes (1988) as having weaknesses and limitations. Giroux has gone as far as charging researchers for contributing to the reproduction of negative racial and gender attitudes and practices:

> The failure to include women and racial minorities in such studies has resulted in a rather uncritical tendency to romanticize modes of resistance even when they contain reactionary racial and gender views. (1983b:287)

Such reactionary racial views cited by Giroux emerge as formidable issues alongside social class issues in such studies as Willis's and MacLeod's.

The main players in Willis's study, the white, working-class lads, perceive and treat racial minorities such as West Indians as "stupid," "thick as a pudding," and "bone headed." Such stereotypical images of racial minorities were often supplemented by staff who perceived the "disconcerting intruder" as "strange and less civilized [than Europeans]...jabbering to each other [talking], and stamping around [dancing]" (p48). The further stereotype of black students' cultural style as aggressive, masculine, and oppositional, as Willis points out, forced their image into conflict with the authority structure of the school.

Similar contemptuous sentiments were directed at blacks by the white, lower-class boys, the "Hallway Hangers" in MacLeod's (1987) U.S. study. His graphic account of racism within a mixed-race neighborhood is captured in one of his white subject's account of a race riot:

> My brothers... were all out there, y'know, stabbin' niggers, beating niggers up. I was brought up thinking niggers suck.... I was brought up to hate niggers (MacLeod, p. 35).

McLeod interprets such violence and antipathy against blacks as an outgrowth of the long-standing tension and resentment rooted in the social and economic conditions of lower-class life in urban America. While researchers cannot be faulted for reporting the reality of race-class antagonisms within schools, work sites, and communities, critics have raised questions about the possible consequences of such reporting. McCarthy and Apple (1988) argue that social class forms of resistance that belittle and negatively stereotype racial minorities carry the potential for confrontation rather than cooperation. Such a behavior of the working class cannot be defined as resistance if it has no transforming qualities. In such cases, class and racial cultures reproduce antagonisms within institutional settings. They compete with each other rather than build solidarity against authority structures in educational, economic, and political systems. Why is this so? The historical and contemporary social factors that give rise to such reactionary racial views are rarely analyzed sufficiently to provide readers with the context in which race-class antagonisms develop. Similarly, as feminist critiques of male, working-class resistance point out, class-gender relations have to be analyzed within a patriarchal structure. Furthermore, McRobbie (1980) finds Willis's emphasis on the sexual exploitation and domination of females by the lads counter productive to any concerted effort to resist the reproduction of class, race, and gender inequality. So the important concluding point here is that a working-class subcultural style of resistance need not be accomplished and romanticized by subordinating females and racial minorities. Any presentation of racial or gender stereotypes in an ethnographic work has to be analyzed within a sociopolitical or historical context.

This study of the Lumberville Jocks has contributed another dimension of race to the resistance theory. It expands on the complex interplay between the Jocks' accommodation to the official achievement ideology and their resistance to the structural patterns of the school to actually achieve education. Historically, the value of education for the black working class has always been perceived in functional terms, as a way of escaping the circumstances of life at the bottom of the socioeconomic hierarchy. Miller's (1976) account of the aspirations of the "lower social strata" Jamaicans in a rigidly class-stratified society described their interest in education solely for social mobility reasons: "To amount to somebody in life"; "to become somebody important in life"; "to be able to get a job and be respected" (p. 63). Working-class Jamaicans and other West Indians emigrate to industrialized countries such as the U.S., Britain, and Canada with the entrenched belief that education is the only vehicle that will transport them up the mobility ladder. In such multiracial societies where the dynamics of race and class are formidable barriers to social advancement, education becomes an even more important means for getting ahead. Through the process of socialization, the black family and the black community rivet into the psyche of the black child the importance of education in the achievement ideology.

This belief in the folk theory of making it applies to blacks in their varied subordinate relationships with the dominant, white group. In the United States, for instance, researchers such as MacLeod found race and ethnicity an important dynamic in the receptivity of the achievement ideology: "ethnicity affects the [black] Brothers' interpretation of their social circumstances and leads to acceptance of the achievement ideology, with all the concomitant results" (p141). Teachers reinforce the belief system of black children that the only way to fulfil the American dream is to "behave yourself, work hard, earn good grades, get a good job, and make a lot of money" (MacLeod, 1987, p. 97). Such a commitment to education would limit their involvement in any form of resistance to schooling. Reinforcing the achievement ideology becomes an effective behavior control strategy for the school's authority structure.

In Britain, West Indian immigrant parents and their second-generation children sought after education as a vehicle for social advancement the same way black Americans do. To provide their children with the much desired educational opportunities, parents have lived and worked under adverse conditions, and have sacrificed their own living standards. In keeping with their parents' folk theory of making it, some second-generation blacks have opted for a life-style that conforms to rather than conflicts with the norms and practices of the school. These status-seeking "mainstreamers," or "mainliners," as Pryce (1978) labeled them, showed no allegiance to the popular "culture of resistance" practiced by black students in the school and community.

The study of the Canadian Jocks has revealed a pattern of commitment to schooling similar to that of blacks in the United States and Britain. What has emerged as a salient feature of this immigrant group at Lumberville is accommodation and resistance as a unitary cultural form. Instead of being overtly oppositional, the Jocks have utilized an ambiguous behavior pattern where conformity and resistance coexist. They drew heavily on ethnospecific forms of behavior as ammunition for resistance and often camouflaged subcultural activities as cultural. Behavior towards authority, whites and females, language forms and communication patterns, style of dress and appearance expressly unacceptable to the norms of the school, were often defended as cultural practices in a multicultural society. The Jocks were thus able to resist forms of schooling they detest, institute subcultural activities as forms of culture, while at the same time maintaining their commitment to the achievement ideology.

Another form of resistance that was often overshadowed by the more overt and rebellious was quiet subversion. The Jocks were also quietly subversive in their repertoire because of its easy interplay with accommodation to schooling. In the ethnography we see the Jocks' skillful manipulation of teachers away from planned lesson presentations to other activities of their liking. They again utilized certain cultural competencies in language, communication, and interactional styles to subvert teacher authority. Giroux points to this potent subversive form of resistance as being often overlooked by researchers.

How has this unique culture of resistance developed among black students in this study? Such complex interplay of accommodation and resistance may be rooted in the history of negative relationships between dominant-group whites and subordinate blacks. Genovese (1974) argues that black slaves [in America] developed cultures of resistance through which they sustained a commitment to liberation. But resistance can be contradictory, implying accommodation to the ruling regime, in contrast to insurrection. As Weis (1985:133–134) analyzes it:

> Resistance and accommodation thus developed as a single pattern in the black community and is reflected on the cultural level of language, notions of time, and work rhythms. These oppositional practices have been lived out and elaborated upon over the years, and constitute core cultural elements in the urban black community today.

Some black, working-class students in white educational settings, by the same token, develop a contradictory relationship toward these institutions, embracing high educational aspirations on the one hand, while falling back on their own subordinate, oppositional culture to resist the structure. This paradox of high educational aspirations and low effort investment packaged with oppositional cultural forms is a significant feature of resistance mediated by race. What motivates the Jocks and other black students at Lumberville to engage in expressions of resistance when such attitudes, behaviors, and actions seriously jeopardize their access to educational opportunities? First, the students' primary socialization outside the school setting occurs within the family and their immediate ethnic community. Within such a social system black children are continually bombarded by expressions of subordination their racial group encounters in interactions with dominant-group institutions. In the job market, black workers recount how thinly veiled employer preference for white workers frustrated their effort to secure employment. Such discrimination in the workplace was usually fronted by the popular excuse "no Canadian experience." For those who gain entry, unequal treatment continues to plague their efforts to achieve equitable working conditions and promotion opportunities with whites. These negative experiences to which children of racial minorities are exposed are not merely perceptions, they are supported empirically by researchers Henry and Ginsberg (1985). Children internalize the negative reactions of their family and community to the denial of housing accommodation of their choice, and in law enforcement they are warned of police vigilance in the surveillance of black youth. The media plays an important role in riveting into the consciousness of black children the feeling of subordination and the need to resist it. Because of this primary socialization process, these students arrive at school with what Fernandes (1988) terms "latent resistance" against institutional structures dominated by whites.

In addition to this gradual external socialization process in which latent resistance develops, black children become a part of the struggle and strategy employed by parents to contest school practices that reproduce them at the bottom of the socioeconomic hierarchy. This study highlights ways in which black parents intervened and subverted Lumberville's tracking mechanism. This primary socialization process within the black family and community fosters within the student a well-developed culture of resistance, one that, unfortunately, conflicts with their folk theory of making it.

The second factor behind the Jocks' culture of resistance may be rooted historically. Blacks of West Indian origin have responded, at whatever cost, to perceived injustices within dominant-culture institutions. While other racial and ethnic groups such as the Punjabis and the Chinese in California (Gibson, 1983; Sung, 1967) may have tolerated prejudice and discrimination in order to benefit from the available educational opportunities, black students resist making such a sacrifice. What factor may be responsible for the differences in response by these minority groups? Ogbu and Matute-Bianchi (1986) refer to the history of the relationship between the minority and the dominant group in question. For example, Chinese immigrants in the United States initially saw themselves as sojourners, temporarily in the U.S. to seek education and wealth and then to return to their homeland and be upwardly mobile. Therefore, it was not in their best interest to overtly contest and oppose the prejudice and discrimination directed at them by the dominant group. Their culture, identity, and language were not overly oppositional, and therefore did not impede their school achievement.

Subordinate minorities such as blacks, on the other hand, have a different history of relationship with the dominant white group in the United States and the West Indies. A history of white superiority and black inferiority in the slave culture followed by black exclusion from full participation in the economic, social, and political life nurtured the development of a black oppositional social identity. Even in slavery blacks developed a culture of resistance that challenged the authority of their oppressors. Today, blacks continue to use this collective identity as a powerful response strategy to the institutional subordination they still face. Unfortunately, Ogbu argues, the repertoire of behaviors, language forms, and identity symbols that black students use in school do not contribute to academic success.

The relationship between blacks of West Indian origin and dominant-group whites in Britain and Canada may be rooted, to some extent, in a similar history of subordination as their counterparts in the United States. Blacks in the West Indies launched major campaigns of resistance against the slave system there, using strategies such as their impenetrable language forms to exclude their oppressors from the communication process, escaping from bondage and returning with reinforcements to free their fellow slaves, destroy property, and wage guerrilla warfare against any authority that opposed them. The eventual abolition of slavery in the West Indies was aided by the resistance movements launched against the system by the slaves themselves. Following the abolition, the black working class continued their struggles against the institutions that sealed them in rigid class-stratified categories.

Emerging from the Jamaican underclass to lead such a struggle was the quasi-religious, quasi-political cult, the Rastafarians. They rejected the existing economic structure of capitalism as an outgrowth of the slave economy and preached instead the doctrine of race and class consciousness, loyalties, and identities as the only way of liberation from white domination. The Black Power movement became popular in the West Indies during this consciousness-raising era. For the Rastafarians, such a resistance was essential because, as Cashmore (1979:214) puts it: "The mechanics of colonialism were thought to perpetuate the obfuscation and militate against the blacks' realization of their own gifts and capabilities." This Rastafarian posture of resistance was exported with emigrants to Britain, Canada, and to a lesser extent, the U.S. and was readily incorporated into the attitudes and behaviors of black working-class youth in these countries. As racial minorities in Britain and Canada, working-class West Indian blacks quickly realized that the dynamic of class as well as the additional dynamic of race were formidable barriers to advancement. Blacks were subordinated in the economic, social, and academic spheres of life within the dominant white culture. They have not, however, accepted this fact of life for themselves and therefore have refused to wait for the passage of time to correct this inequity. Historically, this has not happened for subordinated blacks in the eastern province of Nova Scotia or for native peoples across Canada. So within schools today, black students have rejected "second best" education and have drawn upon their secondary cultural differences to resist the process. To embrace the beliefs, values, attitudes, and behaviors of the dominant culture would compromise their own social identity and the cultural competencies required to survive as a racial minority in a dominant white culture. But by resisting they have jeopardized their own pursuit of school credentials since institutions do not reward cultures that oppose their norms.

Ogbu's analytical concepts are especially helpful in the understanding of the black oppositional culture within the Canadian context. The Jocks' response to schooling moves beyond Ogbu's conceptualization of some immigrants' primary cultural behavior as adaptive and compromising. Instead, they have taken on the secondary cultural differences of resistance and opposition characteristic of castelike minorities within the U.S. The analysis of the Jocks' resistance reveals a culture that is influenced by dynamics far beyond the immediate arena of conflict. From their primary socialization within the home and ethnic community, students arrive at school with the predisposition to oppose the dominant-culture institutions they perceive as racially biased. Such an oppositional frame of reference is not only instigated by the structural regularities of the school and the socializing effects of the primary culture but may be permanently imprinted in the history of negative race relations. Even though the legacy of slavery and its effect on black-white relationships have not evolved the same way as in the U.S., Canada's history of racial discrimination sets the tone for negative intergroup interaction in contemporary society.

Consequently, black, working-class West Indian immigrants with their own legacy of skin color gradation and social class stratification respond uncompromisingly to the Canadian sociocultural structure. They have displayed a posture of resistance to the institutional structures that deprived them of the opportunity to become upwardly mobile. Ogbu's conceptual framework is instrumental in helping us understand the oppositional cultural forms of black, working-class immigrant students in a white school system. The cultural ambivalence of pursuing academic credentials while rejecting the institutional structures that provide such credentials has created a problematic situation. Schools have in place structures and expectations to which they expect all ethnocultural groups with their folk theory of success to adhere. Legitimizing black cultural imperatives into the schooling structure can only come about through a negotiated process. Until there is a mutually agreed upon "cognitive mapping" of where black students expect to go in school and how they expect to get there, the negative interaction between school structures and student cultures will likely continue. The final chapter of this book suggests some starting points for black students to develop emancipatory rather than oppositional strategies, and for schools to reexamine their structures in the view of making them more accommodative to the needs of black, working-class students.

IMPLICATIONS FOR BLACKS IN CANADA

This study has highlighted a group of black, working-class students who in all likelihood will be permanently trapped in an underclass position in Canada's socioeconomic hierarchy. Such marginality is not merely created by institutional factors and student responses to them, but also by powerful external agencies. As marginal workers within the labor market, their services are always at the disposal of others, with the uncertainties of manual and unskilled work and the ever-present threat of joblessness as a forced option. "New" blacks arrived from the West Indies embracing the official achievement ideology or their folk theory of making it in Canada, but they soon recognized some of the contradictions of a meritocratic society and its educational system. Social origin, more so than individual effort, is a key determinant of occupational mobility, and education plays a key role in the transmission of status from one generation to the next. The majority of blacks, therefore, will experience the limits of schooling in realizing their goals and aspirations.

On a more optimistic note, black students' belief in their folk theory of making it, and their own strategies for doing so, confirm their belief in education's emancipatory possibilities. Unlike other working-class cultures that are socialized to accept schooling for unskilled, shop floor jobs, the Jocks in this study have consciously rejected such a future. The implications for such affirmation is that the ideology of achievement through schooling is riveted in the consciousness of these children. Studies such as Sowell (1978) and Foner (1979) have shown remarkable resilience on the part of West Indian immigrants and their children to survive social class and racial inequalities in societies such as the United States, to eventually benefit from whatever educational and economic opportunities were available to them there. Working-class blacks in Canada need to focus on these prospects and possibilities.

THE NEXT GENERATION OF CULTURE AND STRUGGLE

There are already signs among some black youths
despairing of an end to white discrimination, of a
disturbing trend towards a total rejection of white
society and the development of black separatist
philosophies.
(The Scarman Report, 1981:110)

Future research on black cultural forms in Canadian schools and communities need to explore two groups: first-generation black students in higher-track school programs and second-generation blacks of West Indian origin. Such studies should try to ascertain whether the quality and style of black cultural forms in dominant-group schools are influenced by such factors as track placement and generational differences. Studies need to explore and compare some of the cultural forms of high and low-track students. Given Oakes's (1982) exploration of the hypothesis that upper-track students are socialized in a less coercive and less punitive school environment, the expectation is that black students in high-track programs would be less oppositional in their social relations with such institutional structures. Most of the studies of higher-track black students to date have documented their high educational and occupational aspirations. However, few have moved beyond the adjustment framework in analyzing cultural behaviors. This observation of the low-track Jocks revealed their tendency to be at odds with high-track black students and to accuse them of "Uncle Tomming" and "acting white." This hostility is evident in interschool sport competitions among black students from the two tracks. Some higher-track students, by the same token, are believed to disassociate themselves from the postures of resistance and embrace the culture of the dominant group. Research on black culture in both British and United State schools strongly indicates that there is differential commitment to black identity. In Britain, for example, Troyna (1978: 412) reports:

> These [low-track] youths had immersed themselves exclusively in ethnically homogeneous and intra-stream peer groups, and showed both contempt and hostility towards those black pupils in the higher streams.

The black culture in U.S. multiracial schools showed a similar differential commitment to culture and identity. Fordham's (1988) study, for example, explored the strategy of racelessness employed by high-achieving black students to ensure academic success. If future research shows that higher-track black students of West Indian origin respond to schooling in ways that are culturally different from those of low-track students, what may the motivation be for them to do so? Commentators have speculated that higher-track black students do face rigid institutional barriers, but they realize that overt opposition to such structures may only jeopardize their educational and life opportunities. They therefore learn to operate in two cultural frames of reference; behaving according to dominant-group norms when the need arises, and switching to more ethnospecific forms of behavior when the occasion warrants it. Research may establish whether inability or reluctance to alternate between these frames of reference [Ogbu, 1986 defines this as affective dissonance] is a factor in the differential behavior of black students in each track. Any differential commitment to a dissenting ethnic identity and its emerging perspectives carries the potential to fractionalize the black community in urban Canada. The possible emergence of a bipolar community and the implications of such a division for blacks would be an important issue for future research to explore.

This study of the Jocks provides vivid images of the first generation of black West Indians in Canada. Will the second generation embrace the norms, beliefs, symbols, and forms of behavior that may be regarded as cultural continuities of the first generation? British research has highlighted the tendency for some second-generation working-class blacks to separate themselves from the culture of the dominant group—and even from that of their immigrant parents—and identify more with their ancestral subculture. Most attractive to these youths was the Rastafarian subculture and its emphasis on black separatism and a withdrawal from participation in British society. This was their oppositional response to growing up in a school system that marginalized and relegated black culture to an inferior standing. While the immigrant parents of this group were willing to tolerate the denigration of their culture in order to create better life opportunities for their children, the second generation has launched a collective opposition to dominant-group institutions. Cashmore and Troyna (1982:74) write about the British situation: "The movement towards the open defiance and rejection of society suggest massive changes in consciousness [between first- and second-generation West Indian blacks]."

Because working-class West Indian immigrants in Canada have not assumed the tolerant "guest in a foreign land" posture for as long a period as their British counterparts, the difference between the first and second generations may not be as dramatic. Future research should explore the nature of this minority-group culture and determine how such cultural forms impact on educational opportunities and social relations with the dominant group.

Future studies may also focus on the continuity of the folk theory of success from the first to the second generation. Ogbu's (1986:85) theory is that groups, especially minorities, institutionalize in their culture a mapping of how to be upwardly mobile through schooling. From an early age children are socialized into a "cultural conception" of how to get ahead. Black immigrants have articulated this theory of improving their working-class position in Canada's socioeconomic hierarchy. However, the oppositional frame of reference such as that of the Lumberville Jocks appears to be incongruent with the folk theory of making it. Success in school means adopting attitudes and behaviors that are compatible with school norms. Research should explore whether second-generation blacks continue to articulate the need for schooling as a channel for upward mobility. This finding would be revealing since working-class blacks in school systems in Britain and the United States have either drifted progressively into a laissez-faire attitude or have developed an oppositional posture towards schooling.

Except for the historical overview of black schooling in Canada, this study has dealt exclusively with the black cultural forms of recently arrived West Indians. Other groups of blacks have existed for generations as minorities with subordinate status; those in Canada's Eastern province of Nova Scotia is one such group. Research is needed to focus on the cultural aspects of their schooling: the cultural practices they have adopted from the mainstream culture, if any; the survival strategies they have institutionalized within their culture; and the compatibility of their cultural competencies with their folk theory of success. The results of such an investigation will help educational researchers project the future of West Indian blacks in Canada.

CHAPTER 8

Strategies for Change

This ethnographic account of the Jocks and their schooling at Lumberville has highlighted both the institutional and broader societal factors that have given rise to the black culture of resistance and its ongoing struggle with the school's authority structure. Sociologists have always maintained that the school is an arena where dominant-minority group relations in the wider society are played out. Cultural, racial, and class conflicts in the wider society are mirrored within schools since these institutions are not autonomous of the economic, political, and ideological forces operating within society. They promote and transmit the dominant culture and strive to maintain the social relations of the hierarchical and stratified socioeconomic system within the wider society. Subordinate groups whose culture is not consistent with the school's and therefore tend to be marginalized see these institutions as barriers to their development and actively resist their regularities, forms of knowledge, and social practices. This ethnography has shown that subordinate groups respond to these forms of domination with resistance. While this may be instantly gratifying and potentially emancipatory, a misguided oppositional culture is at risk to unsympathetic institutional structures. For schools to reduce structure-culture tensions and represent the interests of dominant as well as minority groups within society, some progressive strategic steps have to be taken. While these strategies will not, in the short term, alter or transform the structural determinants of racial, social class, and cultural subordination in the larger society, they will go a long way in improving dominant-minority group relations within educational settings.

In this closing chapter, we explore strategies for reducing the negative spiraling effects of school structure and student culture and lay the foundation for a more equitable, more democratic school environment. Initially, such strategies may appear to disarm both authority structures and oppositional cultures. In an environment where teachers feel threatened by the actions of students they become wary of embracing strategies that are not power-laden, given their understanding of their position of power and authority within educational settings. By the same token, oppositional students use whatever competencies that they have aquired to participate in the "power play." In the end, the "battle fatigue" experienced by both parties signals the need for interaction mediated by bargaining and trucemaking. In this chapter we explore ways of achieving a conciliatory student-teacher relationship.

The contentious issue of tracking is revisited to explore the development of more culturally appropriate assessment and placement procedures for immigrant and racial minority children. Since employers' racial preference in the workplace sets up barriers in the way of black students preparing for the labor market, a creative strategy of a school-to-work transition will be discussed. Crucial in this school transition process is the realization that sports, a feature of black identity formation, marginalize rather than mobilize the working class in Canada's socioeconomic hierarchy. The chapter concludes with suggestions for movement toward a framework for race equity in education. While race and ethnic relations policies alone cannot change the beliefs and attitudes of the dominant-group teachers and students toward minorities, they may go a long way in guiding intergroup behaviors in educational settings.

WORKING WITH BLACK RESISTANCE

To move toward a pedagogy that provides a democratic learning environment for racial minority students, school personnel need to be equipped with the awareness, sensitivity, knowledge, and skills necessary to structure such an environment. Teachers need to engage in self-examination and raise to the level of consciousness the beliefs, values, and practices they employ in their daily interaction with black students. There has to be an awareness of how racial ideology and practice within society at large affect educational practice in the classroom. This self-monitoring is essential since students, especially black West Indians, as Wolfgang's (1984) research shows, are very perceptive at sensing some teachers' ambivalence toward them. Such a perception usually triggers an antagonistic reaction which is detrimental to the teaching-learning process. School personnel have to be aware of black students' distrustful attitude toward schools, not only because of their own experiences within schools, but also because of their protective socialization within the black community that helps them develop a posture of resistance toward white-dominated institutions. Teachers need to develop the cultural competence and skills to assess the impact of an oppositional social identity on student behavior. How does the dynamic of class, culture, or race influence the way students think and act? Through cultural sensitivity training, valuable insights will be gained into why minority-group students subvert dominant-group values even when such subversion restricts their educational opportunities. Since an understanding of such a contradiction can only be gained through interaction and discourse, teachers need to break down the cultural barriers and communicate meaningfully with students. Giroux (1983) points out that the dialogue is a democratic and institutionally acceptable way of questioning and challenging classroom meanings. Values can be clarified, cultural meanings can be defined, and students can get a better understanding of the structural, social, economic, and political forces that restrict their lives. It is only with such a mutual understanding of structure and culture can teachers and students work cooperatively for change.

The development of cultural competencies also enable teachers to differentiate between the primary and secondary cultural differences of immigrant students. Quite often students camouflage subcultural behavior as ethnocultural, and to avoid censorship declare that they are "simply practicing their culture in a multicultural society." The competent teacher will be equipped to respond appropriately. Since both primary and secondary cultures are dynamic, especially when interacting with the dominant culture, teachers have to be prepared to respond to these changing forms. Without this awareness teachers could easily fall into the trap of working with ethnospecific cultural forms that are static or outmoded. Knowledge that freezes culture in time promotes stereotyping. It is the educator's responsibility to constantly revise preconceived and stereotypical representations of cultural groups within their schools.

Educators need to recognize students' cultural behavior for itself and locate it within its proper sociopolitical context. There has been the tendency of educators to define oppositional or counterschool behaviors as pathological and to seek solutions within the areas of treatment and psychiatry. daCosta's analysis of the behaviors of black adolescents referred to him for psychiatric evaluation and treatment found that students' acts of resistance were responses to sustained racial intolerance and denigration within school and the community. The emancipatory function of the black students' militant posture and group solidarity can easily be invalidated "if they are seen as pathological behaviors" (daCosta 1978:6). Educators therefore need to reevaluate oppositional behaviors in a political context and see cultural resistance as a precondition for long-term changes in school structures.

How should teachers respond to the black youth culture of resistance? Research conducted in multiracial schools finds the tendency for teachers to disapprove of strong ethnic identity, especially among black adolescents. Foster (1986:113) remarks about the American situation, "The pictures of the violence and the disturbances in the ghettos accompanied by racist fantasies linger in the minds of school personnel; many come to school fearful of blacks." In a conflict-ridden environment, student-teacher interactions mediated by fear will be exploited by oppositional students who are constantly exploring ways to undermine, antagonize, and manipulate authority structures they perceive as not serving their interests. Willis (1977:190) suggests strategies for working in conflict-ridden situations:

> Rather than being scared into a moral panic about disruption and violence in the classroom, teachers can place the counterschool culture in its proper social context and consider its implications for its members own long-term future.

Too often school administrators turn to external forces in the face of a challenge from oppositional cultures. Law enforcement personnel—the police, for example—have been instrumental in the maintenance of "discipline machines." This relinquishing of power is usually perceived by students as the staff's inability to cope adequately with student opposition. A long-term effect of such intervention into student-teacher interaction may lead to a negative police-minority group conflict beyond the school and into the community. School personnel should therefore withhold threats or the use of external authority until they have exhausted all school resources available to them. Of course, delinquent behaviors that contravene the law ought to be dealt with by the appropriate law enforcement authorities.

A reexamination of power relations between the authority structure of the school and oppositional students should not lead to the lowering of behavior expectations for students. Urbanski insists, "Overt or subconscious lowering of behavioral or academic standards for any students or group of students would, in itself, constitute the most insidious form of racism" (Foster 1986:xii). Instead of withholding exclusive control over school rules and routines or relying on external authority for support, school personnel need to incorporate marginalized groups in the rule making and rule maintenance process. To achieve this end there has to be a broadening of the dominant-group frame of reference to accommodate the norms, values, symbols, and forms of behavior of minority groups. Reduction of opposition to a structure can only be achieved if minority groups have a vested interest in the system.

School personnel should reduce their domination of the social order by relaxing the rigid structure that exists around the students' time and space. Instead of confining students' free time activities to crowded areas such as the cafeteria, other locations within the school could be made available to those who wish to pursue ethnocultural activities. Such a provision would help reduce the students' open defiance of authority in crowded areas where, in an effort to "save face," staff take punitive action against them. Since the Jocks have used such a forum to aggravate the staff and to challenge the authority structure of the school, opportunities for conflict should be reduced.

As an extension of their progressive stance, teachers should venture from their ethnocentric presentations of dominant-culture knowledge forms and offer a more liberal curriculum that reflects knowledge forms based on the students' own culture and background. As we have seen in chapter 3, the use of Jamaican dialect, for example, has become an issue because of how it was used by students and perceived by the staff. Black students find dialect a functional language form and use it to build group solidarity and to oppose the authority structure of the school. Teachers, by the same token, despise the use of nonstandard language forms because they are excluded from the communication process. This signifies a loss of their authority; they feel threatened by its users, and therefore try to invalidate dialect as an illegitimate language form. Within the context of multicultural education, teachers should revise their attitude toward the dialect forms and use them to achieve a number of cognitive, affective, and behavioral objectives. As a cognitive development exercise, students who are articulate in the dialect could educate their teachers and fellow students by researching and presenting information on such aspects as the origins, vocabulary, and syntax of this Caribbean dialect. Student research may also uncover how the dialect has been adapted and dramatized to achieve desired effects; for example, its adaptation for use by subcultural groups to achieve the effect of subverting the dominant-culture groups. This information-sharing process may lead to knowledge that will decode "patois" and make its meaning more accessible to all. The movement of dialect from the periphery to mainstream curriculum content will undoubtedly increase the self-esteem of the black students who use it, and make them more comfortable with their own culture and heritage. Within the affective domain, dominant-group students will develop an appreciation for this unique language form. At the behavioral level, the learning of patois by the dominant group removes its exclusionary subcultural impact, and encourages its users to utilize more prosocial language forms for communication and self-expression. With this new knowledge base, teachers would be able to develop appropriate strategies when responding to the patois dialect in various contexts.

BLACK SUBCULTURE: FROM OPPOSITION TO CONCILIATION

Throughout this ethnography we were exposed to a black, working-class immigrant group of boys who are committed in principle to the achievement ideology yet engaged in a culture of resistance that makes educational achievement for them problematic. This group was not only in conflict with dominant-group institutional structures, but they have developed relationships with white, working-class boys and working-class females that are antithetical to intergroup solidarity. For black youth to move from their oppositional posture to one of conciliation, they need to assume a politically strategic stance. Such a stance should not in any way compromise, but should strive for a balance between cultural integrity and a struggle for the type of schooling that will afford them greater access to occupational opportunities.

Pressure to conform to a cultural identity and its concomitant norms, values, symbols, and styles of behavior has severely restricted black students' full participation in school life. To set the stage for academic success, black students are encouraged not to operate exclusively in a minority cultural mode. Researchers in Britain, the United States, and Canada have found that school officials are uncomfortable with and disapprove of any display of racial or ethnic identity. In Gillborn's (1988) study of ethnicity and school success in Britain, he found that the black students' conscious strategy was not to emphasize their ethnicity through style of dress and demeanor. To succeed academically, these students acted against the stereotypical images teachers have of them, and when in conflict situations, they accepted criticism without complaint. Fordham's (1988) American study found that black students developed a strategy of "playing down" their identity and assuming a "raceless" persona in order to succeed academically. Within the larger ethnic community these students engaged in culturally sanctioned behaviors and showed group identity. While such a dual allegiance created conflict and ambivalence within these black adolescents, the long-term socioeconomic benefits were substantial.

Black students at Lumberville need guidance to reevaluate their own behavior strategies in light of these research findings. The primary cultural behaviors brought from their country of origin may not, in the long run, impede academic functioning. It is their secondary culture, developed to resist dominant-group subordination, that is most incongruent with striving for academic success. Since these behaviors are defensive strategies that build and protect cultural identity, the Jocks need to develop a delicate balance between pursuing school success and protecting identity. To achieve this, they need in their repertoire alternative ways of responding to conflicts and tensions in dominant-minority group relations. daCosta (1978:6) suggests that adults can be instrumental in helping black adolescents interact with the authority structure through suggestion, persuasion, and practice. These strategies, he continues, should become powerful forces in "developing a healthy scepticism about the motives and attitudes of whites without allowing mistrust and suspiciousness to distort or dehumanize their relationships." Such adult mentors need not come exclusively from the students' own ethnic community but may be identified among the more progressive school staff who recognize the need for empowering oppositional students to work within the established institutional framework.

One of the most crucial relationship issues for the black boys at Lumberville is the gender and race relations they have forged within and outside the school. As we have seen in chapter 4, the Jocks subordinated their female peers by treating them with little or no respect, by restricting the girls' use of the school resources, and by engaging them in sexually suggestive behaviors. Such patriarchal relations might well be an exaggeration of the "cultural hangover" from the West Indies, a male-dominated society. In Canadian society, where gender and race are both subordinated, these boys need to become more conscious of the female's need to rise above male domination. This observed relationship between the two oppressed groups in daily school life is seen as "nonsynchronous," that is, race and gender do not appreciate the need for collaboration instead of competition at a particular point in time (Hicks 1981; McCarthy and Apple, 1988). Black boys, therefore, need to change their domineering attitude and behavior toward females and develop a more democratic and respectful stance toward them. Their experience of white dominance within the Canadian social formation should alert them to the subordination female students experience.

The Jocks' relationship with their white peers also needs improvement. Because of the two groups' limited opportunity to interact voluntarily, they operate almost entirely in separate social systems. Extracurricular sports, an area of common interest, have failed to reduce the social distance. The Jocks have colonized school sports and have strategically marginalized their white peers. By their own feeling of inferiority to blacks in sports, whites have conceded and withdrawn, leaving little or no opportunity for intergroup relationship building. Black and white working-class youth destined for similar positions on Canada's occupational hierarchy need to work cooperatively in breaking down the racial barriers that separate them.

The first step will be to eliminate the stereotypes groups have of each other, especially in the areas of physical and mental ability. Correcting such a belief that blacks are naturally gifted in physical activities while whites are good at academics would gradually remove the barriers that restrict both groups from participating in all areas of schooling. With less identification of school activities with one ethnic group or the other, extreme caution must be taken to ensure that cross-group interaction does not lead to divisive competition.

TRACKING REVISITED

Throughout this study tracking has been one of the most contentious issues for the black community. Parents have revolted against this sorting mechanism that has the potential to reproduce their children at the bottom of the socioeconomic hierarchy. At the center of this controversy is their distrust for the assessment procedures that legitimize the allocation of students to different level programs. This general distrust has led to the parents' reluctance and sometimes outright refusal to have formal assessments that may uncover any disability their children may have. They have argued that, historically, giving school authorities permission to assess is tantamount to committing their children to "dead end" low track school curricula. Such a negative attitude toward assessment and placement procedures is not likely to improve until the system is seen to relocate some of the problems within the socioeducational structure itself.

Samuda (1985:16) identifies some of the problems inherent in the focus of the assessment:

> Psychoeducational assessment which focuses upon the cause of disability and on the remediation of that condition along the lines of the deficit model are pedagogically unsound, humiliating for the student, and frustrating for the teacher.

Samuda and Tingling's (1980) survey of assessment methods used on minority and immigrant children in Ontario schools reveals the traditional classification based on the presumption of internal pathology or deficits. In addition, it is now generally accepted that the so-called "objective tests" are not as "culture free" or "culture fair" as test manufacturers would have us believe. Test materials that are developed and validated on children of a mainstream culture cannot accurately reflect the learning potential and achievement of students from minority cultures. Lynch (1987:75–76) proposes that the form, pattern, and content of all assessments should be free from bias and compatible with the diversity of multicultural societies. When working with immigrants or students from minority cultures, Samuda (1985:137) suggests a comprehensive individual program be developed incorporating the student's level of acculturation, adaptive behavior, primary language, social, economic, and ethnocultural background. The assessment should also be an accurate appraisal of the student's present level of functioning, focusing not on his specific needs only, but also on the particular assets and strengths he brings to the academic situation. Since assessment goes "hand-in-glove" with placement and programming, Samuda insists that assessment should be an ongoing process, and should be a team approach including the teacher, school administrator, counselor or other related professionals.

Ongoing assessment is absolutely essential for immigrant students tested immediately after entry into a school system. Bognar's (1976) research shows the intelligence test scores for a group of black immigrant children increased significantly upon retests. All these students had been assessed initially and placed in special education programs on the basis of their intelligence test scores. When retests indicate the need to upgrade students programs, quite often there are factors such as program maintenance that militate against such a move. These academic judgements become crucial to the students' life chances. Based on these research findings and my own observations at Lumberville, I see great merit in Samuda's comprehensive individual assessment procedures. Data for such an assessment portfolio would be obtained from: classroom teachers' observations; other available school data, possibly from the child's country of origin; dominant language (for the child whose first language is not English, or whose English is of a different dialect); educational assessment including self-report; and intellectual assessment (Samuda 1985:37). The development of such a portfolio takes time and effort; therefore the student's final placement should be delayed until such valuable data are accumulated and evaluated. This strategy serves two purposes: it provides the immigrant student a longer adjustment period, and it gives more time to generate reliable data on which to plan program placement. The Identification, Placement, and Review Committee's (I.P.R.C.)[1] format of gathering data for an assessment portfolio may be adapted for use with immigrant students entering the school system.

A policy for assessing and placing minority-group students is essential for formalizing the suggestions presented here. Essential to such a structure is a professional development component that helps teachers become aware of the bias of culture, provide the skills in test interpretation, and work collaboratively with colleagues and the ethnic community when making judgements about children's futures.

SCHOOL-TO-WORK TRANSITION

The whole area of student transition from Lumberville to the work force needs to be reviewed and expanded. Given such salient issues as the relative uselessness of some credentials to acquire employment, the high rate of unemployment among the school's dropouts and graduates, and the prejudicial attitudes of Toronto's employers toward racial minorities in the labor market, Lumberville needs to address these issues in the way they program, certify, prepare, and introduce their clients to the world of work. Since one of the objectives of Lumberville's school program is to prepare students for the labor market, I suggest that the school expand its human resources and restructure its school-to-work transition program. A larger pool of school personnel is required to prepare students for the work-study experience and cooperative programs, and to seek out and expand the pool of prospective employers on the students' behalf. Employers are not absolved from their own civic responsibility to be nondiscriminatory in their hiring practices. By whatever means available to them, school staff and prospective employers need to develop an innovative partnership that ensures and legitimizes equal access of minorities into the workplace. This intervention against "racial disadvantage" in the labor markets will reduce a black youth's risk of job-seeking frustration and potential unemployment.

In this role, it will be essential to utilize work placement personnel who are not overly constrained by established institutional regularities. Too often classroom teachers do not distribute opportunities to students who engage in the oppositional or counterschool culture. As Willis (1977:187) indicates, vocational guidance counselors have a "different form of attunement to oppositional variants of working-class culture" than classroom teachers, and are frequently more sympathetic to counterculture groups. The findings of this study suggest that counselors must be more willing to offer a realistic appraisal of students' level of achievement within the school, and the quality of their credentials within a competitive labor market, or as entry requirements to institutions of higher learning.

SCHOOL-COMMUNITY RELATIONS

Students from ethnic communities will maximize benefits from an educational system that works in partnership with parents and the community. But this partnership may be difficult to establish for various reasons. Many ethnic and immigrant parents perceive the host school to be a complex and impenetrable institution, and therefore shy away from it. Others see schools as independent of the community, requiring no input, or tolerating no interference from the outside. Despite these perceptions, parents from ethnic communities have varied expectations of schools. These expectations are based on such factors as role patterns, value systems, and cultural characteristics of groups. Hofstede's (1986) research on cross-cultural learning situations found that when students and their parents are raised and "mentally programmed" in cultures that have different value systems than say, Canadians, perplexities arise in classroom interactions. For example, parents from some cultures consider teachers as experts who need not learn anything from lay parents. Yet others come expecting to participate fully in their children's schooling and will feel alienated if they are not provided the opportunity to do so. Teachers, on the other hand, are guided by the norms and the value system of the dominant culture and find it unrealistic to respond readily to the various demands and expectations of the ethnic community. An awareness of what these groups value and how parents may participate in the delivery of what they value will go a far way in building positive school-community relations.

This study has uncovered a number of factors hindering a positive relationship between Lumberville and the black community. Parents express dissatisfaction with the school's unilateral handling of discipline and curriculum matters. Communication with the school, they claim, is one-way, nontransactional, and initiated only at times when the school is reporting disciplinary problems and consequences meted out to their children. Cummins (1986) sees this kind of interaction pattern in association with the power relations that exist between the school and the minority community. This relation is usually a reflection of the disempowerment of such groups in their interaction with societal institutions. The school's authority structure with whom black parents interact at Lumberville appears to be oriented toward the exclusionary end of the collaborative-exclusionary continuum. Here, parental and community involvement in the schooling process are either very superficial or take place on the teacher's terms. Little or no allowance is made for the cultural or institutional factors that restrict parents' participation in schooling.

Teachers, therefore, need to work collaboratively with minority-group parents and their ethnic community as equal partners in education. A crucial area of focus should be that of establishing and implementing standards of operation that consider all cultural groups. Too often, parental and community input is solicited as a reactive rather than a proactive strategy. In the area of program placement, parental involvement will help clarify the discrepancy between parent expectations, student potential, and program placement. More importantly, parents must be alerted to the limits and possibilities of track placements.

OUT OF THE GYM AND BACK TO THE CLASSROOM

Black students in multiracial schools cannot fully benefit from equal educational opportunities until teachers develop a more equalitarian approach to the education of all children, regardless of ethnic or racial origin. To start this process, Cashmore urges teachers to raise their expectations of blacks in intellectual spheres and lower them in relation to "natural sports ability" (1982:210). A useful starting point is for physical education teachers and coaches to make a conceptual distinction between curricular physical education and extracurricular sport programs, since there is the tendency for the latter to encompass the former. Lawson found that when emphasis is placed on athletic performance rather than instruction for all, the highly skilled students easily overshadow the less skilled. These lower-performing students usually develop a complex of inferiority, gradually withdraw, and drop out altogether. A clear separation of physical education from extracurricular sport within the school would help blur the "ethnic territorial boundaries" and foster better intergroup social relations. Lawson concludes that black students could benefit academically since the physical education-sport distinction makes it more difficult for sports to be employed by schools as compensation for academic involvement or social control. Another strategy for reintegrating sport-minded black youth into the academic mainstream is to establish guidelines that restrict year-round involvement in extracurricular sports. Instead of rotating through the year's sport programs, students need to be limited in their activity. To maintain a presence in extracurricular sports, athletes should be expected to maintain a satisfactory standard of academic work. It is essential that academic standards are predetermined and objectively set. Such a predetermination will guard against arbitrary actions of coaches to keep students on school teams, or discourage teachers from using grades as a social control mechanism. These guidelines may be revised for seniors actively preparing for a postsecondary education or career in sport-related or recreational fields.

Teachers should be aware of the impact of school sport on the consciousness of black students. When schools lavish their athletes with sport awards in recognition of their dedication and contribution to the athletic program, sport pursuits are being reinforced at the expense of other facets of school life. Leaman and Carrington (1985) find it ironic that the one area of school life that blacks dominate is, in itself, marginal. To head off this marginality for blacks in the socioeconomic structure later in adult life, school boards should, without reservation, guarantee black students full exposure to the mainstream curriculum. Academic involvement, not sports, is the only passport for working-class blacks up the socioeconomic ladder. This study shows that many black students adopt the sport subculture with dreams of becoming career athletes. The school's responsibility is to sensitize students to the long odds against realizing such a goal. Researchers have documented that thousands of blacks who pursued sports at the expense of academics grew up to be very disillusioned adults. Their awareness that such a preoccupation is not the only prerequisite for a successful career in sport usually comes too late. Without the academic credentials, black youth cannot adjust their goals and assume leadership in related areas such as recreational and community sports. Skills in "playing the game" thus become a nonfunctional commodity in the world of work. Edwards (1988) claims that over ninety-five percent of high school athletes do not play competitively after leaving school. By emphasizing this harsh reality, teachers will help to jolt black students out of the false consciousness that a career in sport is a viable option for them. In this regard, career counselors should serve as a resource in seeking out and providing vital information on which students can make informed career choices.

To increase awareness about the precarious world of sport, the school may launch additional initiatives. They may invite both well-established as well as would-be athletes to share their experiences with students on such topics as the meagre success rate of high school athletes making it to the ranks of paid career athletics; the academic sacrifices made to pursue sports; the potential long-term effect of limited academic exposure; the athletic expectations of college scholarship donors and the academic value of "jock courses," those programs without academic rigor designed to help athletes move through a college career without failure. Such a revealing dialogue will provide insights into the precarious life of those who invest too heavily in sports.

Coaches, perceived as one of the most influential socializing agents in the life of the black athlete, have to assume some responsibility for rerouting these students. Instead of overinvesting in black athletes and designating them the "work horses" of the school's sports program, coaches ought to encourage and build a more racially diverse pool of athletes. This will achieve two ends. First, it will release black students to integrate into other areas of social life; and second, students of other racial and cultural groups who had surrendered this area to blacks will return to participate equally in extracurricular sport activities. Some critics are convinced that if classroom teachers invest a comparable amount of time developing the academic skills of black students as coaches spend developing their athletic skills, black students will achieve academically as they do athletically.

Finally, black parents have to be vigilant in monitoring the use of their children's time in school. They need to communicate a strong message to teachers to relinquish the ideology that guides the differential development of black students for the dubious world of sports and white students for predictable futures in attainable jobs. If parents believe in the achievement ideology and status mobility through schooling, then they must encourage in their children the appropriate academic attitudes and behaviors to achieve these ends. The black community has always worked in partnership with the school in rewarding the accomplishments of the black athlete. Similarly, the black community needs to collaborate with the school in seeking out and publicly recognizing black students who have achieved academically. This recognition need not be undertaken only at the national level with grand award ceremonies, but also at the local community level where more students stand a chance at public recognition. It is only by improving the profile of academic accomplishments that it will compete with sports for a high profile among black students.

TOWARD A FRAMEWORK FOR RACE EQUITY IN EDUCATION

Black students in white dominant school structures have not benefited from Canada's policy of multiculturalism. This policy, declared over two decades ago, was designed to promote and reflect the cultural and racial diversity of Canadian society, and acknowledge the freedom of all members of Canadian society to preserve and share their cultural heritages. Despite this national policy, dominant-group educators continue to embrace an ethnocentric approach to pedagogy within schools. A lack of commitment to antiracist multicultural relations is partly responsible for the failure of some school districts to effectively launch their policy initiatives.[2] For those teachers committed to the dominant mainstream culture, their assimilationist ideology is quite evident in statements that urge the assimilation of ethnic minorities into the mainstream and discourage endeavors that develop the awareness, knowledge, and skills of a staff to function effectively in a racially and ethnically diverse school population.[3]

Although the official policy is multiculturalism, these responses show that the dominant teaching paradigm within Canadian classrooms is cultural assimilation. Teachers are socializing racial and ethnic minority children into the dominant, mainstream culture. Since assimilationist views are essentially incongruent with multiculturalism, the endeavors of those who are uncommitted are usually "folkloric," tokenistic, and celebratory in multicultural education practices. The celebration of ethnic festivals, holidays, and carnivals, the parading of ethnic customs, the playing of ethnic music, the preparation of ethnic foods all constitute cultural "life-styles" rather than "life chances." In Western societies such as Britain, the United States, and Canada, the controversy over racializing educational policies is more divisive than debates over ethnicity and culture. Troyna and Williams (1986) have documented the British experience and have provided a substantive guide for policymakers planning to deal with the dynamic of race in education. Already in Canadian classrooms there are expressions of resistance and the establishment of defensive barricades to any form of antiracist education. Efforts to raise awareness to the impact of racism on the educational opportunities of black students are discouraged on the grounds that scholastic buildings are becoming " racism identification centers." Since the attitudes, expectations, and actions of school personnel are key factors in the academic success or failure of the black child, any policy intervention to improve the life chances of this racial minority must address such personnel.

To summarize, any framework for improving the schooling of black, working-class students at institutions such as Lumberville must incorporate strategies that address the structure, culture, and the politics of schooling. Here, I restate some of the most crucial issues with suggestions for change. The cultural competence of teachers is challenged when confronting ethnospecific oppositional cultures of students. A high level of competence may only be developed through understanding, interacting, and immersing oneself in such cultures. To perceive and deal with student cultures from an ethnocentric perspective is to overlook their political significance. By the same token, black students need to move beyond their oppositional social identity and adopt a more conciliatory stance when negotiating change to school structures. In this regard, a positive and equitable working relationship with other groups of students who are white, working-class, and female will help create the partnership needed to effect change.

In the area of student assessment and track placement, movement away from the deficit model to evaluations that capitalize on the child's own knowledge base and past learning experiences will help teachers focus on the potential that remains untapped by standardized tests based on dominant-group students learning experiences. For blacks to benefit from schooling, the structure and the content of tests must focus on both their strengths and needs. While in school, getting black students out of the gym and back into the classroom means moving them from a marginal to a mainstream curriculum. Both teachers and parents have to ensure that black youth invest more time and effort in academic rather than athletic endeavors. This change of emphasis will greatly improve their life chances.

A school program that prepares students for the world of work needs school personnel to help negotiate work placements for racial minority students. For black school leavers to enter a job market that discriminates on the basis of race, the schools need a mechanism to break down such barriers. This will undoubtedly foster a smoother transition from school to work, and reduce the growing number of black unemployed youth. Good school-community relations are essential for students to maximize their learning experiences. Honest, open communication is a key ingredient of such a partnership, especially when the interaction is cross-cultural and with "new" immigrants that did not themselves experience the Canadian school system. "Cultural brokers" that liaise between the school and the ethnic community are initially indispensable, but it will be the school, parents, and the community that are ultimately responsible for developing and maintaining constructive interrelationships.

APPENDIX A

Research Methodology

> (I)ndividuals have meaning structures that determine much of their behavior. The research seeks to discover what these meaning structures are, how they develop, and how much they influence behavior...
> (Wilson 1977:254)

My employment of qualitative research methods for studying black culture at Lumberville is based on the hypothesis that the way people behave is influenced by their social reality. The ethnographic approach utilizing participant observation as its key mode of data collection provides an insider's view of how institutional structures and student cultures interact. Essential to ethnographic research is the perspective of the interpretation that is brought to bear on the actions and behaviors of the observed. My interest in the cultural perspective was influenced by Willis's (1977) qualitative look at how and why a group of British working-class boys produced a culture that was counter-school, and in the long run, reproduced social inequality within British society. His pioneering work on this class-based subculture provided the methodological framework for the study of other student subcultures informed by such dynamics as race and gender.

My research agenda for studying black culture in a Canadian high school thus involved entering the research site and establishing my role—collecting, recording, analyzing and interpreting the data, and relating these findings to current sociological theories in education. The field study was conducted over a two-year period (from mid-1983 to early 1985). Gaining access was an involved process of negotiation with school and district administrators at various levels within the system's hierarchy. Initial discussion with the school staff on the effects of subcultural behavior on educational opportunities led to a more formal conceptualization of the research problem when negotiating entry into the school. References to emerging studies from Britain (Willis, 1977; McRobbie, 1978; Fuller, 1980) and the U.S. (Everhart, 1983; Weis, 1983) raised the issue of students' cultural orientation

129

as a hindrance to their educational progress and positive social relations in school. Given the multicultural nature of the student population and the prominence of West Indian subcultural activities within Lumberville, my request to study its effects on educational opportunities was well received by the administrators. Teacher responses to the study varied from reserved interest to hostile interrogation. Why show preferential treatment to blacks by studying them? Why not study whites too? Why not do the research at other schools with a higher percentage of blacks? Some teachers suggested that I study black girls because they seem to have difficulty with interpersonal relationships. This mixed reaction to my proposed study prepared me for a cautious entry into my fieldwork.

Beyond the initial gatekeeping process, some teachers volunteered their help in identifying cliques they perceived as suitable subjects for my research. Quite often, those groups recommended were the "main trouble-makers" and their members on frequent suspensions from school. I exercised caution in deciding on a group and followed Bogdan and Taylor's (1975:44) advice: "Don't let subjects (or school officials) tell you whom, what, or when to observe."

The black group for study was identified only after lengthy observation of the multirace school population, and the various subgroups within it. The cohesive nature of the group, its common Jamaican heritage, its intense involvement in school sports [from whence the label "Jocks" was ascribed], and its members' and their parents' belief in social mobility through schooling, made this group ideal for the study. My access to the in-group was enabled by my demonstrated interest in their sporting life. More importantly, by being black and of West Indian background, the Jocks accepted my presence without reservations. Access to their parents was negotiated through the students themselves. Initial contacts with the parents were followed up by in-depth, face-to-face interviews.

The research approach in collecting data was multimodal, utilizing such techniques as participant observation, unstructured, open-ended interviews, and the examination of student and school documents. Participatory observation varied on a continuum from observation to participation, and became the chief strategy for collecting data. Here, I was immersed in the perspective of the Jocks by sharing in their day-to-day experiences in school and in their larger community. My major focus was on the Jocks' interaction with each other, with other students in the class, and with the teacher. Guidelines for my classroom observation, were informed by the work of Spalding (1982). These helped me to focus on aspects of teacher control approaches and student oppositional behaviors in the classroom. More specifically, I zeroed in on four essential areas of the interactional processes in the classroom: student oppositional behaviors, teacher control strategies, teacher-student relationships, and student-peer relationships. In observing student oppositional behaviors in the classroom, I centered on such counterschool activities as flaunting school rules, resisting the teacher, negative attention-seeking, delaying instruction, and avoiding school work. My observation of teacher control strategies in the classroom focused on the ways in which the teacher reminded and redirected students regarding limits, the amount of teacher time and effort spent on student discipline and behavior, and the strategies used by teachers to ensure rule following by students.

In the area of academic interactions between the teacher and students, I monitored the types of opportunities students had for constructive participation in lessons. For example, were students actively involved in class discussions, research assignments, etc., or did the teacher ask for the recall of low-level facts or information? I also monitored whether the level of student involvement in academic tasks determined students' off-task behaviors. Also monitored were positive and negative interactions of teachers and their students. Positive interactions included the teachers' use of humor in the teaching-learning process, and their expression of enthusiasm in their interactions with students. I also monitored the teacher maintenance of his/her authority position and control within the school, and their protection of social boundaries with students. The fourth essential area of observation was student-peer relationships and the quality of interactions and cooperation among different subgroups within the school. Here I explored such information as classroom dissonance, cliqueishness, competitiveness, and friendliness among individuals and groups of students. Observation was focused on the degree to which such groups as black students use seating arrangements, language, and communication patterns to strengthen their cliques and alienate white students.

Outside the classroom, observations continued in the hallways and corridors, the cafeteria, the gymnasium, locker rooms, and on the playground. My presence in various settings and at the school's special events provided me with a more complete picture of the Jocks' cultural forms both at school and within the community at large. I observed the Jocks as they participated in interramural as well as major interschool sport tournaments at other school sites around Metropolitan Toronto and adjacent regions. Other special events that yielded data were the school's graduation ceremonies where valedictorians received certificates, diplomas, and other awards before moving into the labor market, and the school's open house events when the school communicates with the community through its displays and exhibits. Participant observation at school dances yielded significant data on both the leisure pursuits of the Jocks and their indulgence in the more oppositional elements of their subculture.

The interview was the next most important source of data. Ellen (1984) describes the ethnographic interview as a conversation in which "ethnographers risk the appearance of naïveté and ignorance in order to satisfy themselves that they have understood what is being said, and risk wandering up blind alleys in order to confirm the validity of the ways in which they are beginning to make sense of their data" (p. 226). This type is called "the open-ended interview" and was used extensively throughout the data collection phase of this research. Interviews were not limited to the Jocks, but included other students as informants, as well as teachers, administrators, coaches, and parents who all contributed to the formation of useful constructs, or opened access doors to the collection of more data. On occasions when the Jocks were interviewed as a group, the format was essentially informal, with the boys utilizing their own distinctive form of association and group dynamics to contribute. I utilized in these group interviews what Bullivant (1987:52) labels "dialectical questioning," that is, making an effort to generate a dialectic between group members by "posing general questions, feigning ignorance and even claiming wrong knowledge," to the point where respondents even get into arguments in an attempt to correct the interviewer or put forth their own point of view. It was at such "rap sessions" that important cleavages of opinions, attitudes, and values emerged. While I acknowledge some of the drawbacks of group interviews,—for example, chorusing, and the domination of the group by the articulate speakers—these sessions became important social events for the Jocks because, as researchers such as Furlong (1984), Kochman (1972), and Head (1979) have found out, "rap sessions" complemented the interactional style typical of black working-class males.

Primary data collected through participant observation and interviews were further supplemented and corroborated by secondary documentary data. These ranged from curriculum and program implementation guidelines to Board directives and other administrative guidelines to schools and within-school documents such as course selection guides and codes of behavior for students.

Other relevant within-school information included such correspondence as absence and detention lists, "do-not-admit" (student to class) lists, and general administrative-type correspondence from the school office to classroom teachers regarding day-to-day routines and regularities. Curricular materials, handouts in class, samples of students' work, student diaries, the student newspaper, and student report cards provided important insights into the quality of the curriculum and student work. This category also contains cocurricular events such as open house, graduation ceremonies, and fundraising events. This multimodal datagathering process using participant observation, elicitation interviews, and information from relevant records and documents about Lumberville contributed significantly to a fuller understanding of the school setting.

Field notes were specific, factual, and as descriptive as could be conveniently recorded without interfering with my participation in the setting. In addition to copiously written field notes, a tape recorder, still pictures and a video camera were utilized throughout the fieldwork to record data in a comprehensive and authentic way. Individual interviews, group discussions, and playground interactions during athletic competitions were recorded on audio tape and later transcribed for analysis. Such low-inference narratives and the mechanical recordings of such data significantly increased their reliability. To preserve the anonymity of the participants, no photographs are included in this publication. In addition to my use of pseudonyms to protect the identity of the participants, I opted for more generalized accounts of particular events when more specific descriptions would have revealed the identities of the informants.

Validating data was done mainly by triangulation: that is, comparing and cross-checking the consistency of information derived from different sources, at different times, using different modes of data collection (Denzin 1978). Triangulation did produce some inconsistencies in the data, but efforts were made to explain these in the analysis stage. Generally, there was consistency in the overall patterns of data and this contributed significantly to the credibility of the findings. There are factors such as selection criteria and sampling to consider when generalizing findings of qualitative research. While quantitative research emphasizes the measurement of responses and does require a large input to generate a representative sample for generalizability, qualitative methodologists, on the other hand, are more interested in the meanings that subjects attach to their actions (Gordon 1984). In the Lumberville study, the selection of the Jocks for study was not based on random sampling. The Jocks as a cultural entity within the social system of the school existed before the study. They were identified and selected for study because of the distinct social and cultural forms they lived out from day-to-day. In addition, the size of the group, a nucleus of eight boys, is of little significance to me as an ethnographer operating within the cultural studies framework. In defense of Willis's small number of "lads" and the issue of generalizability, Gordon (1984:110) points out that "the lads constitute both sample and population." Willis (1981) himself indicates that particular features of his subjects could be generalized to other groups within other schools.

In the Lumberville study, the Jocks' cultural forms have features that can also be generalized to other black student subcultures in other multiracial schools in Canada, the U.S., and Britain. The status of the research setting may also raise questions about the study's translatability. Early in the fieldwork phase of the study, Lumberville High was classified as a "special" rather than a "typical" high school in terms of its program and clientele. A government regulation, however, upgraded its status in the latter stage of the fieldwork, making it more like a typical high school. This change of status was mainly administrative and had no immediate significant impact on the school's institutional structures, its program offering, or its clientele. The cultural forms of students such as the Jocks remained essentially the same as they were before the school's program was reclassified. So in terms of the study's translatability, the school structure,as well as the students' cultural forms within it, parallel those of other low-track schools. The findings of this study not only permit some generalization, but also serve as a basis for further qualitative research on black culture and struggle in other multiracial school settings.

ANALYSIS AND INTERPRETATION OF DATA

Analyzing data was not an activity relegated entirely to the postfieldwork stage of the research. Recording, validating, and analyzing data were carried out simultaneously in a spiral fashion: initial data were recorded; validation processes then required further data collection to confirm already gathered material, or to clarify contradictions discovered. When emerging themes were common enough, I engaged in "theoretical sampling." This meant seeking out and accumulating materials from all sources that were related to the emerging themes such as the Jocks' opposition to, and separation from, the mainstream culture. From these themes tentative hypotheses were formulated. As Gordon (1984) indicates, theory-free research is a myth. The theoretical assumptions that researchers bring to each study help them make sense of the data they accumulate. In my Lumberville study, my theoretical and empirical support came from the broader framework of schooling, reproduction, and resistance theories. I interpreted the Jocks' oppositional cultural forms as resistance to the reproduction of the social inequality generated by schooling at Lumberville and in the society at large. As children of black, working-class parents at the bottom of Canada's socioeconomic hierarchy, a schooling structure and curriculum such as Lumberville's have the potential to reproduce this social division of labor.

However, the reproduction and resistance theories did not adequately address aspects of resistance that were so potent in the culture of the Jocks. Because of the theory's analytic inadequacy, I had incorporated other perspectives for looking at the data. For example, Ogbu's (1987) theoretical approach to minority schooling views their postschool opportunity structure as a factor that inhibits good school performance and behavior. Ogbu also differentiated the distinctive cultural features of immigrant minorities, and elaborated on how the various cultural forms impact on the quality of schooling they receive. The dimensions interlock well with other theories in explaining how the Jocks' oppositional attitudes, behaviors, and actions resist the reproductive structural determinants of Lumberville.

Central to any reproduction and resistance framework is the structuralist-culturalist debate. Here I drew on Giroux (1983), Apple (1982), and Weis's (1985) frameworks to analyze the interactive process of Lumberville's institutional structures and the Jocks' oppositional cultural forms. I utilized these complex but interlocking theories to adequately explain the data at hand, and to make projections as to the Jocks' destiny in Canada's social division of labor.

To summarize, the research process outlined here has highlighted the use of ethnographic techniques to get an insider's view of black cultural forms in schools. By observing and interpreting the responses of the marginalized to the structures of the institution, this inquiry process provided new insights into patterned cultural behaviors within schools. In order to preserve the holistic perspective of the ethnomethodologist, extreme care was taken to accurately present the social discourse of the main players and other informants, and while doing so, locating these transactions within a theoretical framework. Quantz and O'Connor (1988:108) remind the ethnographic researcher:

> ...Marginalized people do not create a culture isolated from the social forces of power and history. [This recognition] is essential to our understanding of culture as it affects our educational institutions.

Immigration Selection Criteria:
A Summary of the "Points System"

FACTORS	CRITERIA	MAX. POINTS
1. Education	One point for each year of primary and secondary education successfully completed.	12
2. Specific Vocational Preparation	To be measured by the amount of formal professional, vocational, apprenticeship, in-plant or on-the-job training necessary for average performance in the occupation under which the applicant is assessed in item 4.	15
3. Experience	Points awarded for experience in the occupation under which the applicant is assessed in item 4 or, in the case of an entrepreneur, for experience in the occupation that the entrepreneur is qualified for and is prepared to follow in Canada.	8
4. Occupational Demand	Points awarded on the basis of employment opportunities available in Canada in the occupation that the applicant is qualified for and is prepared to follow in Canada.	15

5. Arranged Employment or Designated Occupation	Ten points awarded if the person has arranged employment in Canada that offers reasonable prospects of continuity and meets local conditions of work and wages, *providing* that employment of that person would not interfere with the job opportunities of Canadian citizens or permanent residents, and the person will likely be able to meet all licensing and regulatory requirements; *or* the person is qualified for, and is prepared to work in, a designated occupation and meets all the conditions mentioned for arranged employment except that concerning Canadian citizens and permanent residents.	10
6. Location	Five points awarded to a person who intends to proceed to an area designated as one having a sustained and general need for people at various levels in the employment strata and the necessary services to accommodate population growth. Five points subtracted from a person who intends to proceed to an area designated as not having such a need or such services.	5
7. Age	Ten points awarded to a person 10 to 35 years old. For those over 35, one point shall be subtracted from the maximum of ten for every year over 35.	10
8. Knowledge of English and French	Ten points awarded to a person who reads, writes, and speaks English *or* French fluently. Fewer points awarded to persons with less language knowledge and ability in English or French.	10
9. Personal Suitability	Points awarded on the basis of an interview held to determine the suitability of the person and his/her dependants to become successfully established in Canada, based	10

on the person's adaptability, motivation,
initiative, resourcefulness, and other
similar qualities.

10. Relative   Where a person *would* be an assisted   5
                                relative, *if* a relative in Canada had
                                undertaken to assist him/her, and an
                                immigration officer is satisfied that the
                                relative in Canada is willing to help him/her
                                become established but is not prepared, or
                                is unable, to complete the necessary formal
                                documentation to bring the person to Canada,
                                the person shall be awarded five points.

                              POTENTIAL VALUE   100

NOTES:

1. Initially, a minimum of 50 points were needed for consideration for admission to
   Canada. However, an immigration officer may approve or reject an immigrant
   regardless of the number of points obtained if, in his or her opinion, the points do
   not accurately reflect the applicant's chances of successfully establishing him or
   herself in Canada.

2. Over the years, the selection criteria and points requirements have been adjusted to
   respond to Canada's national requirements and the qualifications of the applicants.
   The immigration policy was never static.

SOURCES:

Canada Manpower and Immigration. *The Immigration Program* Ottawa: Information
Canada, 1974; *Highlights from the Green Paper on Immigration and Population.*
Ottawa, 1975.

Notes

CHAPTER ONE

1. Rastafarianism is a quasi-religious, quasi-political cult that emerged from the urban underclass of Jamaica during the 1930s and 40s. Their beliefs were that colonialism and white capitalist structures are responsible for blacks' socio-economic subordination. Oppressed blacks should therefore reject the values, norms, and lifestyles of the white, class-stratified society and establish their own egalitarian, Afrocentric way of life. They demonstrate this ideology in their demeanor, language, and life-style, and utilize reggae music to disseminate their subversive, oppositional messages. Aspects of the Rasta life-style and ideology have had a tremendous influence on black youths' culture of resistance in countries such as Britain; these will be elaborated upon throughout the book.

CHAPTER TWO

1. Here we are referring mainly to the West Indians from countries that were formerly still British colonies: Jamaica, Trinidad & Tobago, Barbados, Guyana, Antigua, St. Kitts–Nevis, St. Lucia, Dominica, Monsterrat, and St. Vincent.

2. The formal procedure for dealing with surplus teachers in a declining student population is formulated in the terms and conditions of employment between teachers' federations and boards of education. While other factors are taken into consideration, seniority is the key in this procedure: a teacher displaced elsewhere within the school district could, in turn, "bump" a less senior teacher at Lumberville.

CHAPTER THREE

1. This perspective emphasizes the utility and politics of language in sections of Britain's black community (Fisher 1983).

2. While in the United States southern creole has been gradually modernized and is disappearing from use (Genovese 1974), Jamaican creole has scarcely been affected by this modernizing trend (Bagley 1979). Since black students at Lum-

berville refer to their language form as "patois" instead of the more correct "Jamaican creole," the two terms will be used interchangeably throughout this book.

3. The more volatile sociopolitical conditions in Jamaica make the messages in "rebel music" potentially dangerous there. In Canada, however, the social and institutional structures have not provided the conditions whereby "rebel music" may empower blacks to engage in active militant behavior. Second-generation blacks and their likely change in consciousness may respond actively to the oppositional messages of rebel music as their British counterparts have done.

4. It has become the practice of some patrons to carry concealed weapons such as guns when attending parties such as the ones described above. These armed party-goers are often referred to as gunmen.

CHAPTER FOUR

1. Serving five eight-fifteens means a student is detained from 8:15 A.M. for five days instead of starting school at the usual 9:00 A.M.. Weston rebelled against this consequence, and, according to him, was immediately served with a harsher penalty, a suspension.

2. The school office in many high schools has earned the reputation of being the area where students are kept in a holding pattern until their turn arrives for them to face the "executioner."

3. Example of such immigrant jokes would be that Jamaican immigrant students who do not behave in class will be given a one-way ticket back to Jamaica.

CHAPTER FIVE

1. Players from Father Henry's (private Catholic) school hockey program stand the chance of being drafted by junior leagues from which professional teams recruit players.

2. Adjustment was made later to Lumberville's extracurricular sports program to accommodate "collegiate" soccer. This gave the Jocks the opportunity to compete with students from higher-track collegiates.

3. In basketball, one of the fastest growing and most popular high school sports in Ontario, black students dominate both quantitatively and qualitatively. For example, the two most successful schools in provincial championship and tournaments field all-black or almost all-black squads (CBC's "Inside Track").

CHAPTER SIX

1. More recently, school administrators have instituted a policy of delaying any standardized assessment of new immigrants until they have been in the school system for a minimum of two years. This moratorium is in effect in many school jurisdictions with immigrant populations.

2. This quote is from a brief presented to the Lumber Valley School Board by a community-based group advocating for better education for minority and working-class students.

CHAPTER EIGHT

1. These Identification, Placement, and Review Committees (IPRC) are mandated by the Ontario Ministry of Education to help each school district identify exceptional students and programs for them. These data gathering and placement deliberation processes are very comprehensive, covering exceptionalities such as behavioral, communicational, intellectual, physical, and multiple.

2. An independent review of multicultural and race relations initiatives carried out by the Toronto Board of Education showed a serious lack of leadership at the administrative level (Hitner Starr Associates, 1985). This lack of commitment is also evident in other school jurisdictions in Canada and abroad (Troyna and Williams, 1986; Bullivant, 1987).

3. Teacher responses to a survey on race and ethnic issues in education. Preservice and inservice teachers often chose an assimilationist position over other approaches such as integration or multicultural and antiracist education when working with minority-group students. Such positions are expressed in surveys and follow-up discussions.

Bibliography

Abella, R. *Equality in Employment. A Royal Commission Report.* Toronto: Commission on Equality in Employment, 1984.

Adair, D., and J. Rosenstock. "Interracial Attitudes in Ontario Schools." *O.T.F. Interaction* (April 1977):6–7.

Adair, D., and J Rosenstock. *Multiculturalism in the classroom: A Survey of interracial attitudes in Ontario.* Toronto: Federal Department of the Secretary of State, April 1976.

Anderson, W. W., and R. W. Grant. *The Newcomers: Problems of Adjustment of West Indian Immigrant Children in Metropolitan Schools.* Toronto: York University, 1975.

Apple, M. W. *Education and Power.* Boston: Routledge & Kegan Paul, 1982.

Apple, M. W., and L. Weis. "Ideology and Practice in Education: A Political and Conceptual Introduction." In *Ideology and Practice in Schooling,* edited by M. Apple and L. Weis. Philadelphia: Temple University Press, 1983.

Armanino, D. C. *Dominoes.* New York: David McKay Co. Inc., 1973.

Bagley, C. "A Comparative Perspective on the Education of Black Children in Britain." *Comparative Education* 15, no. 1 (1979): 63–81.

Bailey, B. *Jamaican Creole Syntax; A Transformational Approach.* Cambridge: Cambridge University Press, 1966.

Baldwin, J. "If Black English isn't a Language, Tell Me What is?" *Roots* 1, no. 4 (1979).

Barret, L. A. *Adolescent Deviance: An examination of the Phenomenon among Black West Indians in Toronto.* Master's thesis, University of Toronto, 1980.

Billingsley, B., and L. Muszynski. *No Discrimination Here? Toronto Employers and the Multi-racial Work Force.* Toronto: Urban Alliance on Race Relations and The Social Planning Council of Metro Toronto, 1985.

Bogdan, R., and S. J. Taylor. *Introduction to Qualitative Research Methods.* New York: John Wiley and Sons, 1975.

Bognar, Carl J. "West Indians, I.Q., and Special Education Placement." *Orbit* 7 (April 1976).

Bourdieu, P., and J. C. Passeron. *Reproduction in Education, Society and Culture.* Beverly Hills: Sage, 1977.

Bowles, S., and H. Gintis. *Schooling in Capitalist America.* New York: Basic Books, 1976.

Brake, Mike. *The Sociology of Youth Culture and Youth Subcultures.* London: Routledge & Kegan Paul, 1980.

Bullivant, B. M. *The Ethnic Encounter in the Secondary School: Theory and Case Studies.* London: Falmer Press, 1987.

Calliste, A. M. "Educational and Occupational Expectations of High School Students." *Multiculturalism* 5, no. 3 (1982):14–19.

Canada Manpower and Immigration. *Highlights from the Green Paper on Immigration and Population.* Ottawa, 1975.

———. *The Immigration Program.* Ottawa: Information Canada, 1974.

Carby, H. V. "Schooling in Babylon." In Centre for Contemporary Cultural Studies, *The Empire Strikes Back.* London: Hutchinson, 1982.

Carrington, B. "Sports as a side track. An analysis of West Indian involvement in extra-curricular Sports." In *Race, Class and Education,* edited by L. Barton and S. Walker. London: Croon Helm, 1983.

Carrington, B., and E. Wood. "Body talk: images of sport in a multi-racial school." *Multi-racial Education* 11, no. 2 (1983):29–38.

Cashmore, E. "More than a Version: a study of reality creation." *British Journal of Sociology* 30, no. 3 (1979):307–321.

———. "Black Youth, Sports and Education." *New Community* 10, no. 2 (1982):213–221.

Cashmore, E., and B. Troyna. (eds.) *Black Youth in Crisis.* London: Allen and Urwin, 1982.

Census of Canada. *Catalogue 92–810 and 95–826.* Ottawa: Statistics Canada, 1976.

———. *Catalogue 95–936 (3–A) and E5654.* Ottawa: Statistics Canada, 1981.

Christiansen, J. M., A. Thornley-Brown, and J. A. Robinson. *West Indians in Toronto: Implications for helping professionals.* Toronto: Family Services Association, December 1980.

Cummins, J. "Empowering Minority Students: A Framework for Intervention." *Harvard Educational Review* 56, no. 1 (1986):18–36.

daCosta, G. A. "Orphans and Outlaws: Some impacts of racism." *Multiculturalism* 2, no. 1 (1978):4–7.

Denzin, N. K. *The research act: A theoretical introduction to sociological methods.* New York: McGraw Hill, 1978.

Dhondy, F. "The Black Explosion in the Schools." *Race Today* 4 (June 1974).

Driver, G. "Cultural Competence, Social power and School Achievement: A case study of West Indian pupils attending a secondary school in the West Midlands." *New Community* 5, no. 4 (1977):353–359.

Edwards, H. "The Single-minded Pursuit of Sports Fame and Fortune is Approaching an Institutionalized Triple Tragedy in Black Society." *Ebony* 43, no. 10 (August, 1988):138–140.

Ellen, R. F., (ed.) *Ethnographic Research: A Guide to General Conduct.* London: Academic Press, 1984.

Equality Now. *Report of the Special Committee on Visible Minorities in Canadian Society.* Ottawa: Canada House of Commons, issue no. 4 (March 1984).

Everhart, R. B. *Reading, Writing and Resistance.* Boston: Routledge & Kegan Paul, 1983.

Fernandes, J. V. "From the Theories of Social and Cultural Reproduction to the Theory of Resistance." *British Journal of Sociology of Education* 9, no. 2 (1988):169–180.

Fine, M. "Examining Inequity: View from Urban Schools." Unpublished Manuscript, University of Pennsylvania, 1982.

Fisher, G. "Language in a political context: the case of West Indians in Britain." *Oxford Review of Education* 9, no. 2 (1983):123–131.

Foner, N. *Jamaica Farewell: Jamaican Migrants in London.* London: Routledge & Kegan Paul, 1979.

———. "West Indians in New York City and London: A Comparative Analysis." *International Migration Review* 13, no. 2 (1979): 281–297.

Fordham, S. "Racelessness as a Factor in Black Students' School Success: Pragmatic Strategy or Pyrrhic Victory?" *Harvard Educational Review* 58, no. 1 (1988):54–84.

Fordham, S., and J. Ogbu. "Black Students' School Success: Coping with the 'Burden of Acting White'." *The Urban Review* 18, no. 3, (1986): 176–206.

Foster, H. L. *Ribbin', Jivin', and Playin' the Dozens: The Persistent Dilemma in our Schools.* 2nd ed. Cambridge: Ballinger, 1986.

Fuller, Mary. "Black girls in a London Comprehensive School." In *Schooling for Women's Work,* edited by Rosemary Deem. London: Routledge & Kegan Paul, 1980.

———. "Young, Female and Black." In *Black Youth in Crisis,* edited by E. Cashmore and B. Troyna. London: Allen and Urwin, 1982.

Furlong, J. "Black Resistance in the Liberal Comprehensive." In *Readings on Inter-action in the Classroom*, edited by S. Delamont. London: Methuen, 1984.

Genovese, E. *Roll, Jordan, Roll: The World the slaves made*. New York: Pantheon Books, 1974.

Gibson, M. A. *Home-School-Community Linkages: A Study of Educational Equity for Punjabi Youths*. Final Report. Washington, D.C.: The National Institute of Education, 1983.

Gillborn, D. A. "Ethnicity and Educational Opportunity: Case Studies of West Indian male-white teacher relationships." *British Journal of Sociology of Education* 9, no. 4 (1988):371–385.

Gilmore, P. "'Gimme Room': School resistance, attitude and access to Literacy." *Journal of Education* 167, no. 1 (1985):111–128.

Giroux, H. *Ideology, Culture and the Process of Schooling*. Philadelphia: Temple University Press, 1981.

———. *Theory and Resistance in Education: A Pedagogy for the Opposition*. Massachusetts: Bergin & Garvey, 1983a.

———. "Theories of Reproduction and Resistance in the New Sociology of Education: A Critical Analysis." *Harvard Educational Review* 53, no. 3 (1983b):257–293.

Goldlust, J., and H. A. Richmond. *A multivariate analysis of the economic adaptation of immigrants in Toronto*. Toronto: York University, 1973.

Gordon, L. "Paul Willis—Education, Cultural and Social Reproduction." *British Journal of Sociology of Education* 5, no. 2 (1984):105–115.

Griffin, Christine. *Typical Girls?* London: Routledge and Kegan Paul, 1985.

Hall, S. *The Young Englander*. London: National Committee for Commonwealth Immigrants, 1967.

Hall, Stuart, and Tony Jefferson, (eds.) *Resistance through Rituals*. London: Hutchinson, 1976.

Hallinan, M. T., and S. S. Smith. "The effects of classroom racial composition on students' interracial friendliness." *Social Psychology Quarterly* 48, no. 1 (1985):3–16.

Hannerz, U. *Soulside: Inquiries into Ghetto Culture and Community*. New York: Columbia University Press, 1969.

Hargreaves, A. "Resistance and Relative Autonomy Theories: Problems of Distortion and Incoherence in Recent Marxist Analyses of Education." *British Journal of Sociology of Education* 3, no. 2 (1982):107–126.

Hargreaves, D. *Social Relations in a Secondary School*. London, Routledge & Kegan Paul, 1967.

Harvey, E. G. *Program and Organizational Review of Secondary School Occupational and Vocational Programs*. Unpublished report. Toronto: Ontario Institute For Studies In Education, 1980.

Head, W. "The West Indian Family in Canada: Problems of Adaptation in a Multiracial, Multicultural Society." *Multiculturalism* 3, no. 2 (1979):14–18.

Head, W. and J. Lee. *The Black Presence in the Canadian Mosaic*. Toronto: Ontario Human Rights Commission, 1975.

Hebdige, D. "Reggae, Rastas and Rudies." In *Resistance through Rituals,* edited by S. Hall and T. Jefferson. London: Hutchinson, 1976.

Henry, F. "The West Indian Domestic Scheme in Canada." *Journal of Social and Economic Studies* 17 (March 1968):83–92.

———. *The Dynamics of Racism in Toronto: A Report*. Ottawa: The Department of the Secretary of State, 1978.

Henry, F. and E. Ginsberg. *Who gets the Work*. Toronto: The Urban Alliance On Race Relations and Metro Toronto Social Planning Council, 1985.

Hicks, E. "Cultural Marxism: Nonsynchrony and Feminine Practice." In *Women and Revolution,* edited by L. Sargent. Boston: South End Press, 1981.

Hitner Starr Associates. *Race Relations Program Review*. Toronto: Toronto Board of Education. December, 1985.

Hofstede, G. "Cultural Difference in Teaching and Learning." *International Journal of Intercultural Relations* 10, no. 3 (1986):301–320.

Ijaz, M. A. *Ethnic attitudes of elementary school children toward Blacks and East Indians and the effect of a cultural program on these attitudes*. Ed.D. thesis, University of Toronto, 1980.

Ikulayo, P. "Physical Ability and Ethnic links." *British Journal of Physical Education* 13, no. 2 (1982):47.

Kane, M. "An assessment of Black is Best." *Sports Illustrated* 34, no. 3 (1971):72–83.

Kochman, T. (ed.) *Rappin' and Stylin' Out: Communication in Urban Black America*. Urbana: University of Illinois Press, 1972.

Larter, S., M. Cheng, and E. N. Wright. *Streaming in Toronto and Other Ontario Schools*. Toronto: Toronto Board of Education, 1980.

Lawson, H. "Physical Education and Sport in the Black Community." *Journal of Negro Education* 48, no. 2 (1979): 187–195.

Leaman, O., and B. Carrington, B. "Athleticism and the reproduction of gender and ethnic marginality." *Leisure Studies* 4, no. 2 (1985):205–217.

Li, P. S. "The Stratification of Ethnic Immigrants: The Case of Toronto." *Canadian Review of Sociology and Anthropology* 15, no. 1 (1978):21–40.

Louden, D. "Self-esteem and the Locus of Control: some findings on Immigrant Adolescents in Britain." *New Community* 7, no. 2 (1978):218–234.

Lowe, K. "Dialect and Identity." *TESL talk* 12, no. 3 (1981): 17–22.

Lynch, J. *Prejudice Reduction and the Schools.* London: Cassel Educational Ltd., 1987.

MacLeod, J. *Ain't No Makin' It: Leveled Aspirations in a Low-income Neighborhood.* Boulder, Colo.: Westview Press, 1987.

Marotto, R. A. *Posin' to be Chosen: An ethnographic Study of Ten Lower-class Male Adolescents in an Urban High School.* Ed.D. dissertation, State University of New York at Buffalo, 1977.

McCarthy, C., and M. Apple. "Race, Class and Gender in American Educational Research: Toward a Nonsynchronous Parallelist Position." In *Class, Race and Gender in American Education,* edited by L. Weis. Albany: State University of New York Press, 1988.

McLaren, P. *Cries from the Corridor: The New Suburban Ghettos.* Toronto: Methuen, 1980.

———. *Schooling as a Ritual Performance: Towards a Political Economy of Education Symbols and Gestures.* London: Routledge & Kegan Paul, 1986.

McPherson, B. D. *Minority Group Socialization: An Alternative Explanation for the Segregation by Playing Position Hypothesis.* Paper presented at the Third International Symposium on the Sociology of Sport, Waterloo, Ontario, Canada, 1970.

McRobbie, Angela. "Working-class Girls and the Culture of Femininity." In *Women Take Issue,* edited by the Centre for Contemporary Cultural Studies, Women Studies Group. London: Hutchinson, 1978.

———. "Settling Accounts with Subcultures: A Feminist Critique." *Screen Education* no. 34 (Spring 1980).

Miller, E. "Education and Society in Jamaica." In *Sociology of Education: A Caribbean Reader,* edited by P. M. E. Figueroa and G. Persaud. Oxford: Oxford University Press, 1976.

Mullard, C. *Race, power and resistance.* London: Routledge & Kegan Paul, 1985.

Multicultural Residents' Committee. *School & the Community: Parental Perceptions & Involvement Report.* Submitted to the 'Lumber Valley' School Board, Toronto, 1985.

Oakes, J. "Classroom Social Relationships: Exploring the Bowles and Gintis Hypothesis." *Sociology of Education* 55 (October 1982):197–212.

———. *Keeping Track: How Schools Structure Inequality.* New Haven: Yale University Press, 1985.

Ogbu, J. U. *The Next Generation: An Ethnography of Education in an Urban Neighborhood.* New York: Academic Press 1974.

———. "Variability in Minority School Performance: A Problem in search of explanation." *Anthropology and Education Quarterly* 18, no. 4 (1987):312–334.

Ogbu, J. U., and M. E. Matute-Bianchi. "Understanding Socio-cultural Factors: Knowledge, Identity and School Adjustment." In Bilingual Education Office, *Beyond Language: Social and Cultural Factors in Schooling Language Minority Students.* Los Angeles: Evaluation, Dissemination and Assessment Center, California State University, 1986.

Ontario Human Rights Commission. *Life Together: A report on Human Rights in Ontario.* Submitted to the Council for Metropolitan Toronto by the Task Force on Human Relations. Toronto: The Task Force, 1977.

———. *The Experience of Visible Minorities in the Work World: The Case of M. B. A. Graduates.* Toronto, 1983.

Ontario Ministry of Education. *Ontario Schools: Intermediate and Senior Divisions (O.S.I.S.) Program & Diploma Requirements.* Toronto: 1984.

Parsons, T. "The School class as a social system: some of its functions in American Society." *Harvard Educational Review* 29 (Fall 1959):297–318.

Petroni, F. A. "'Uncle Toms': White Stereotypes in the Black Movement." *Human Organization* 29, no. 4 (1970):260–266.

Pineo, P., and J. Porter. "Occupational Prestige in Canada." *Canadian Review of Sociology and Anthropology* 4 (1967):24–40.

Porter, J. *The Vertical Mosaic: An analysis of Social Class and Power in Canada,* Toronto: University of Toronto, 1965.

Pryce, K. *Endless Pressure.* Harmondsworth: Penguin, 1978.

Quantz, R. A., and T. W. O'Connor. "Writing Critical Ethnography: Dialogue, Multivoicedness, and Carnival in Cultural Texts." *Educational Theory* 38, no. 1 (1988):95–109.

Radwanski, G. *Ontario Study of the Relevance of Education and the Issues of Dropouts.* Toronto: Ontario Ministry of Education, 1988.

Ramcharan, S. "Special Problems of Immigrant Children in the Toronto School System." In *Education of immigrant Students: Issues and Answers,* edited by A. Wolfgang. Toronto: Ontario Institute For Studies In Education, 1975.

———. "The Economic Adaptation of West Indians in Toronto, Canada." *Canadian Review of Sociology and Anthropology* 13, no. 3 (1976):295–320.

Rex, J. "West Indian and Asian Youth." In *Black Youth in Crisis,* edited by E. Cashmore and B. Troyna. London: Allen and Urwin, 1982.

Rist, R. C. "Student social class and Teacher expectation: The self-fulfilling Prophecy of Ghetto Education." *Harvard Educational Review* 40, no. 3 (1970):411–454.

Roberts, K., J. Duggan, and M. Noble. "Racial Disadvantage in Youth Labour Markets." In *Race, Class and Education,* edited by L. Barton and S. Walker. London: Croon Helm, 1983.

Rosaldo, M. Z. and L. Lamphere. "Introduction" In *Woman, Culture, and Society,* edited by M. Z. Rozaldo and L. Lamphere. California: Stanford University Press, 1974.

Rosenbaum, J. E. *Making Inequality: The Hidden Curriculum of High School Tracking.* New York: John Wiley & Sons, 1976.

Roth, J. *West Indians in Toronto: The Students and the School.* Toronto: Board of Education for York, 1974.

Ryan, W. P. *Blaming the Victim.* New York: Vintage, 1976.

Samuda, R., and W. Tingling. *The Use of Tests in the Education of Canadian Immigrants: Building on Strengths or Deficits?* Kingston: Queen's University Press, 1980.

Samuda, R., and A. Wolfgang. (eds.) *Intercultural Counselling and Assessment.* Toronto: Hogrefe Inc., 1985.

Scarman, Rt. Hon. Lord, *The Brixton Disorder*, 10–12 April 1981. (Cmnd.8427) London: Her Majesty's Stationery Office, 1981.

Selden S. "Eugenics and Curriculum: 1860–1929." *The Educational Forum*, 43 (1978):67–82.

Siggin, M. "To this cold place: Reggae, Rastas, Racism and Dreams of an Island in the Sun." *Toronto Life Magazine* (March, 1981):34–76.

Solomon, R. P. "Dropping out of Academics: Black Youth and the Sports Subculture in a Cross-National Perspective." In *Dropouts From School: Issues, Dilemmas and Solutions,* edited by L. Weis, E. Frarar, and H. G. Petrie. Albany: State University of New York Press, 1989.

Sowell, Thomas (ed.). *Essays and Data on American Ethnic Groups.* Washington, D.C.: The Urban Institute 1978.

Spalding, R. L. "Teacher Activity Recording Schedule (Short Form) and the Coping Analysis schedule for Educational Settings (Short Form)." *Journal of Educational Research* 76, no. 1 (1982):7–13.

Sung, B. L. *Mountain of Gold: The Story of the Chinese in America.* New York: Macmillan, 1967.

Tanner, N. "Matrifocality." In *Woman, Culture and Society,* edited by M. Z. Rosaldo and L. Lamphere. California: Stanford University Press, 1974.

Tepperman, L. *Social Mobility In Canada*. Toronto: McGraw-Hill-Ryerson, 1975.

Troper, H. "The Creek-Negroes of Oklahoma and Canadian Immigration, 1909–1911." *Canadian Historical Review* 53, no. 3 (1972):272–288.

Troyna, B. "Race and Streaming: A Case Study." *Education Review* 30, no. 1 (1978): 59–68.

———. "Differential Commitment to Ethnic Identity by black youth in Britain." *New Community* 7, no. 3 (1978): 406–414.

Tyack, D.B. *One Best System: A history of American Urban Education*. Cambridge, Massachusetts: The Harvard University Press, 1974.

Walker, J. W. *West Indians in Canada*. Ottawa: Canadian Historical Society, 1984.

———. *Racial Discrimination in Canada: The Black Experience*. Ottawa: The Canadian Historical Association, Historical Booklet no 41, 1985.

Weis, Lois. "Schooling and Cultural Production: A Comparison of Black and White Lived Culture." In *Ideology and Practice in Schooling,* edited by M. Apple and L. Weis. Philadelphia: Temple University Press, 1983.

———. *Between Two Worlds: Black Students in an Urban Community College*. Boston: Routledge & Kegan Paul, 1985.

———. "Seeing Education Rationally: The 'Bottom' and the 'Top.'" *International Journal of Sociology and Social Policy* 6, no. 2 (1986): 61–73.

Willis, Paul. *Learning to Labour: How working-class kids get working-class jobs*. Westmead, England: Saxon House, 1977.

———. "Cultural production is differnt from cultural reproduction is different from social reproduction is different from reproduction." *Interchange* 12, no. 2 (1981):48–67.

Wilson, S. "The Use of Ethnographic Techniques in Educational Research." *Review of Educational Research* 47, no. 1 (1977):245–265.

Wilson, W. J. *The Declining Significance of Race: Blacks and Changing American Institutions*. Chicago: University of Chicago Press, 1978.

Winks, R. W. *The Blacks in Canada: A History*. New Haven: Yale University Press, 1971.

Wolfgang, A. The Development of an Inter-racial Facial Recognition Test: Phase III. *A comparison between new Canadian West Indian and Canadian sensitivity to inter-racial facial expressions and social distance*. Toronto: Ontario Institute For Studies In Education, 1980(a).

Wood, C. "Among Saints and Swingers: Defining the Social Work Task in Relation to West Indian Lifestyles." *Social Work Today* 5, no. 7 (1974):213–215.

Wright, E. N. *Students' Background and its Relationships to Class and program in School (Every Student Survey).* Toronto: Toronto Board of Education, 1970.

Wright, E. N., and G. K. Tsuji. *The Grade 9 Student Survey, Fall 1982* Research Project No. 174. Toronto: Toronto Board of Education, 1984.

Index

155